Legal Self-Help Guide

Will, Trust, & Power of Attorney

Creator and Estate Records

Organizer

Legal Self-Help Guide

Will, Trust, & Power of Attorney
Creator and Estate Records
Organizer

Sanket Mistry, JD, MIA, edited by J.T. Levine, JD, MFA

Peerless Legal

ISBN 13: 978-1-940788-00-5
ISBN 10: 1-940788-00-5
Library of Congress Control Number: 2013922338

Mistry, Sanket
Will, Trust, & Power of Attorney Creator and Estate Records Organizer: Legal Self-Help Guide
First Edition
Peerless Legal | Roanoke, Virginia | www.PeerlessLegal.com

™ and Peerless Legal are trademarks of PeerlessLegal.com.

Peerless Legal books are available for special promotions. For details, contact Peerless Legal by email at sales@peerlesslegal.com, or visit www.PeerlessLegal.com.

While the author has made every effort to provide accurate telephone numbers and internet addresses at the time of publication, neither the publisher nor author assume any responsibility for errors or changes that occur after publication. The publisher does not have any control over, and does not assume any responsibility for, author or third-party websites or their content.

This publication is designed to provide accurate and authoritative information in regard to the subject matters covered. It is sold with the understanding that the publisher and author are not engaged in rendering legal, accounting, or other professional services. If legal advice or other expert assistance is required, the services of a competent professional should be sought.

From a *Declaration of Principles jointly adopted by a Committee of the American Bar Association and a Committee of Publishers*

THIS PRODUCT IS NOT A SUBSITUTE FOR LEGAL ADVICE.
Disclaimer required by Texas statutes.

DISCLAIMER

Laws change constantly. Every effort has been made to provide the most up-to-date information. However, the author, publisher, and any and all persons or entities involved in any way in the preparation, publication, sale, or distribution of this publication disclaim any and all representations or warranties, express or implied, about the outcome or methods of use of this publication, and assume no liability for claims, losses, or damages arising from the use or misuse of this publication. All responsibilities for legal effects or consequences of any document prepared from, or action taken in reliance upon information contained in this publication are disclaimed. The reader should not rely on this author or this publisher for any professional advice. Users of this publication intending to use this publication for preparation of legal documents are advised to check specifically on the current, applicable laws in any jurisdiction in which they intend the documents to be effective. Make sure you are using the most recent edition.

Is This Legal Self-Help Guide for You?

The Peerless Legal mission is to empower individuals by giving them legal self-help tools. The Legal Self-Help Guide series was created as the embodiment of that mission.

The goal of this Guide is to provide you with the information you need to understand your legal rights and responsibilities. In doing so, we hope you will be able to resolve your legal issues yourself or know enough to feel confident in your decision to hire a licensed attorney. This Guide provides a meaningful alternative to most of the books in law libraries. Peerless Legal's goal is for you to be able to understand this material.

You are not alone in choosing self-help. Everyone faces legal issues at some point in their life. While most of us have the capacity to understand our legal rights and responsibilities, finding good legal information can be daunting. As the costs associated with legal representation rise, more and more people are opting to take certain legal matters into their own hands.

In this Guide, Peerless Legal provides you with meaningful alternatives to costly legal representation for legal issues you can handle yourself. This Guide is a plain-English alternative to the legal jargon that fills most legal books.

This book is for you if:

- you want to handle your own legal issues,
- you are not sure whether the legal issue you are facing merits the high cost of an attorney,
- you are in the process of looking for competent, legal representation, but are unsure how to evaluate legal services,
- you have retained an attorney and are unsure whether your attorney is competently handling your legal issues,
- or you want to know more about a specific legal topic.

It is important to manage expectations when acting on your own behalf or with an attorney. The forms in this book may differ from the forms that are commonly used in your local jurisdiction. You can check local rules by going to the court's website, making a phone call to the office of the clerk of court, or by visiting a local law school library. Generally, law school libraries serve as Federal repositories and are open to the public during normal business hours.

Warning There are some legal issues that seem simple and straight forward, but in reality only an attorney with extensive experience on the issue would know there is an inner-tangling.**

Acknowledgments

This book has been nothing short of a group effort. In addition to the above named dedication, I would like to thank most J.T. Levine for her gift of editing.

About the Author

Sanket Mistry earned his JD from the Walter F. George School of Law at Mercer University. He is a member of the New York State Bar and author of several books in the Legal Self-Help Guide series. He has worked, and volunteered, at a number of nonprofits, government agencies, and for-profit corporations. He also holds a BA in philosophy from Emory University and an MIA from Columbia University. He is an avid traveler and tennis player.

About the Editor

J.T. Levine earned her JD from the Walter F. George School of Law at Mercer University. She has edited several books for Peerless Legal. She is a member of the Georgia Bar. Prior to law school, she earned an MFA in Professional Writing from the Savannah College of Art and Design and a BA from the University of Miami. She is an animal lover and has a pharaoh hound named Tut.

Table of Contents

1. People
   A.   My Information
   B.   Beneficiaries
   C.   Guardians for Minor Child
   D.   Pets
   E.   Others Who Depend On Me
   F.   Witnesses and Notary Public
   G.   Executor

H.   Trustees

2. Property
A.   Real Estate
B.   Bank Accounts
C.   Insurance and Annuities
D.   Death Benefits
E.   Trusts
F.   Non-Real Estate Debt
G.   Retirement Accounts and Pensions

3. Other Things
A.   Organ, Tissue, and Body Donation
B.   Inform the World of Your Death
    a)   Cremation or Burial, and Funeral and Memorial Services
    b)   Newspaper Obituary Information

ASSIGNMENT OF PROPERTY TO A LIVING TRUST
AFFIDAVIT OF ASSUMPTION OF DUTIES BY SUCCESSOR TRUSTEE
LIVING TRUST AMENDMENT
REVOCATION OF LIVING TRUST

I. Introduction

This book will help you get your estate in order so that you can successfully create your own legal estate documents. It includes information about wills, trusts, power of attorneys, and other common estate planning information. This book is not intended to be read as a novel. It is intended to be used as a reference guide. Pay attention to headings because they are your guide-posts. This book is laid out in a way to help you find information quickly.

This book is written in plain-English with as little legal jargon as possible. However, sometimes the legal jargon cannot be avoided. Where legal jargon is used, there is a plain-English explanation that accompanies it. If you need addition explanations, refer to the Glossary.

By the time you finish reading this book, you should be able to:

- successfully understand how to, and create, your own legal documents,
- know enough about your issue to determine whether it's complicated enough to warrant hiring an attorney, and
- understand your legal rights and responsibilities.

The book begins with a vast array of legal information that will help you create your estate documents. The information is a broad overview. Not every piece of information will pertain to you or to your jurisdiction. More information about your jurisdiction is available online at the web addresses provided in the back of this book in the Appendix.

There is an introduction section at the beginning of each of the major topics. Think of this as a preview of what is to come. Then there are detailed explanations of the important legal issues. Next, there is an estate records organizer to help you to get organized. It will also allow the executor of your estate to easily find important information. You should complete as much of the organizer as possible. It can become part of your estate upon your death, but is not required to be a part of your estate. Next, we have provided a check-list and sample legal forms. The check-list will help you make the sample form legal. There are additional explanations after the sample legal forms that tell you what you should do with the legal forms after you completed them. The reminder of the book is devoted to the Appendix that includes State Specific Information, Glossary, and Index. The State Specific Information provides links to information on each of the 50 states and the District of Columbia. Laws in different states vary and you should review this section to find your specific state rules. The Glossary provides definitions to common legal terms. The Index provides cross-references.

The tools in this book will provide you with the legal information you need to create your own estate documents or to equip you with the information you need to hire a competent attorney.

II. Wills

1. Introduction to Creating Your Own Will

Do you know what will happen to your house or bank accounts after you die? What would happen to your stuff if you were in a comma? Do you want to make sure that your spouse, children, or other family members are taken care of after you die? Have you considered what you would say to loved ones in a heart-to-heart message to help them deal with your death? Do you want to make a will? This section helps you to do all of these things.

This section provides the instruction and information you need to create your own will. Creating your own will allows you to:

- control how your property will be legally disturbed when you die,
- name someone with the legal authority to follow and fulfill your wishes in your will,
- name someone to take care of your minor children,
- name someone to manage the property you leave for your minor children,
- leave a letter to your loved ones, and
- create a living will to govern what medical procedures you want or do not want if you should become terminally ill.

Most people know what a will is, generally, and know that they should have one. With the right information and good judgment, most people can create their own legal will. If you picked up this book, you want to prepare a simple will yourself or you want to learn more about wills so that you can successfully communicate your specific needs to an attorney.

The following chart shows the steps to create your own will using this book. The wills section is also organized in this layout.

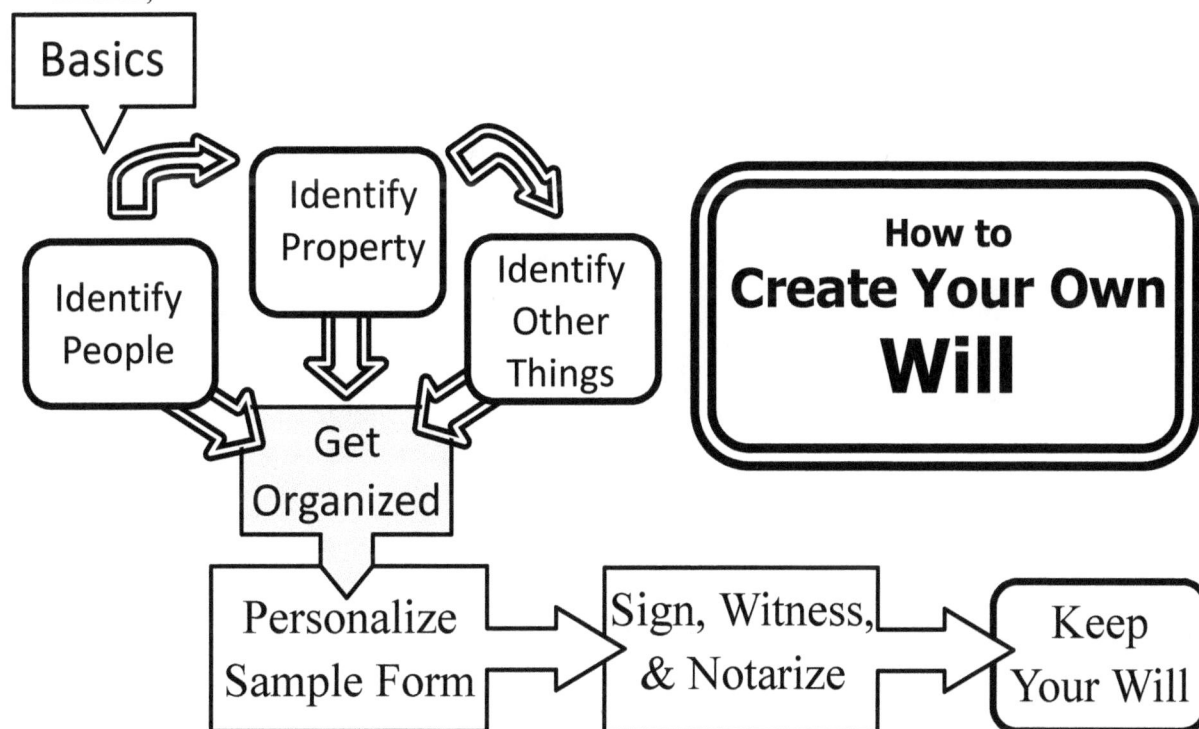

Basics

Identify People

Identify Property

Identify Other Things

Get Organized

How to **Create Your Own Will**

Personalize Sample Form

Sign, Witness, & Notarize

Keep Your Will

2. Basics—Functions and Uses of Wills

As you prepare to create your will the first step you need to take is to understand what a will is and why you are creating it. This chapter takes you through the basics of why you need a will and how a will can assist you in preparing to identify who will get what when you die. Along with explaining the basic functions of a will, this chapter will help you determine what you need to include in your will, and what, if any, additional resources you might need.

A. What Is a Will?

There are many kinds of wills. But, in short, a *will* is a written document that controls how your property will be disturbed when you die, who will serve as guardians of your minor children (and who will take care of the minor children's property until they reach 18), and how your property will be managed upon your death. The person whose property is affected by the will is called the *testator*. If it is your will, you are the testator.

One of the primary advantages of creating a will is that you control how your property will be distributed when you die and/or how your children will be taken care of.

Most wills created are now typed, but this is not always required. One option is to handwrite your will. A handwritten will is called a *holographic will*. A holographic will may be allowed so long as it's written entirely by your hand, signed, and dated. No witnesses are required. Not all states recognize holographic wills. Where recognized, judges, generally, disfavor them because they are often incomplete or considered unreliable documents.

An *oral will*, which is a will that is spoken, is only valid in a handful of states. Note that even where valid, there are still very specific rules. Generally, an oral will is really not a will at all.

A will that is held only electronically is called an *electronic will* and is only valid in Nevada. Although there may be a trend towards using them in the future, for now, Nevada is the only state that recognizes electronic wills. There are some added requirements for an electronic will.

Many people, including lawyers, put outdated legal jargon in a will, but it adds no extra meaning or authority to the will. Avoid such language if you don't understand it. Chances are, if you fully understand your will, then so will the judge. If you don't understand your will, then it is likely that a judge won't understand your will either. Do yourself a favor and write a will you understand.

B. Who Can Create a Will?

In general, almost anyone can create a will. The size and value of your estate is not a factor in determining if you can create a will. To legally create a valid will you need to be of:

1. legal age, and
2. "sound mind."

a) Legal Age

The legal age to create a will is usually 18, but some states have a lower age limit. For example, the lower age limit in Georgia is 14 and in Louisiana it is 16. If you are under the legal age, but in the military or married, many states allow you to create a will.

b) "Sound Mind"

A "sound mind" requires that, at the time that you *execute* the will (i.e., when you sign and date your will), you:

- know what a will is, what it does, and that you are creating a will,
- name beneficiaries that have a relationship to you that you understand, and
- you understand the nature and extent of your property.

If you meet these requirements, then the judge is not likely to ignore (set aside or disregard) your will for lack of a "sound mind." If you can understand the concept of a "sound mind," you are probably of "sound mind."

C. How to Create a Will?

The purpose of the will governs how the will is created. A will is a written document stating your wishes. The document must be signed by you, the testator, and witnessed by at least two other people (three in Vermont). The will can be changed, modified, or revoked prior to your death. The will can be probated upon your death. To be a legal will, it must go through a process known as *probate*. Probate is where the court distributes your property to the beneficiaries you name in your will or as governed by state law.

At a minimum, a will must:

1. include at least one statement giving away property or naming guardians for minor children who have no parents,
2. be signed and dated by the testator, and
3. be signed and dated by two witnesses (except in Vermont which requires three witnesses).

It is useful to also name an *executor* in your will. An executor is a person, named by you in your will, to manage your estate after you die. Some states call the executor a *personal representative*. An executor may also be referred to as an *administrator*.

D. What Makes a Will Valid?

A will is not valid until it has been approved by probate court. In determining whether your will is valid, the court will apply the laws of the state of which you are a resident (except for real property, see next paragraph). You should create your will to be probated in the state where you are a resident. This does not mean that you have to be physically present in that state when you create your will. You can specify in your will, what your state of residence is. Generally, when a will is determined by a court to be valid in one state, then it is valid in all of the other states. If you are temporarily overseas when you create your will, your residence will be the state of your permanent residence. If are permanently overseas because you have taken on another country's citizenship or given up your U.S. citizenship then this book will not meet your needs.

When it comes to *real property*, that is real estate, the laws of the state where the property is located will govern.

E.   What a Will Can Do for You

Just as there are multiple types of wills, there are multiple things a will can do, depending on your testator's relationship to your survivor's.

You can give property to individuals after you die. In doing so, you do not necessarily need to be even handed. You can give a greater share to your best friend and less to your neighbor.

You can appoint someone to handle your estate for you, called an *executor*, which is a person named by you in your will to manage your estate after you die. Some states call the executor a *personal representative* or refer to them as an *administrator*. The executor can:

- gather together all your property and distribute them according to your will,
- file paperwork for taxes or probate forms,
- hire any necessary professionals, such as attorneys or accountants,
- have the power to sell your property, and
- take other actions without having to get a court order.

A will can be used to name guardians for your minor child(ren). Naming guardians for your minor child(ren) will avoid long custody battles and allows you to have some control over who raises your minor child(ren).

If you do not want your property to be distributed immediately upon your death, you can designate in your will for the executor to create a *trust* for the child(ren) at a later date. A trust is a legal relationship where one person or entity holds legal title to, and has responsibility for, property for the financial benefit of another person or entity.

You can direct the executor to create a trust to decrease estate taxes. You can also decrease certain estate taxes by doing a more complicated estate plan. As a practical matter, if your estate is valued at or more than $2 million, then it makes sense to create a trust for the sole purpose of decreasing certain estate taxes. For this, you should seek the services of a professional.

F.   What a Will Cannot Do for You

Limitations on a will are things in your will that, no matter what you write, will not be enforced by the courts. The main limitations on a will are that a will cannot be used to conduct illegal activity and cannot put unreasonable conditions on inheriting property.

Illegal activity is anything that is unlawful to do in the state where the will is probated. Any provision in your will that violates a state or Federal law will be struck down. If too many of these provisions are included in your will, then a court might see this as evidence that you lacked a "sound mind" when you created your will, especially if the provisions are obvious in their illegality.

You are allowed to put reasonable conditions and restraints on an inheritance. For example, you can instruct your executor to only pay your daughter if she graduates from college.

An example of an unreasonable restraint is a restriction you write into your will that only allows a person to inherit if they do something that is against public policy, including permanently restricting a person's right to transfer, sell, or enjoy the property. So, if the executor can pay your daughter only if she agrees to divorce her husband, that is an unreasonable restraint and the provisions will be ignored by the courts.

Permanent restrictions on inheritance in a will are not allowed. For example, if you will your car to your neighbor only if he agrees to never drive it on a Sunday, the court will not allow this provision in your will. However, you may include a restriction if you include a time limit on the restriction. So, if instead you write that your neighbor is not allowed to drive the car on Sundays for the next year that may be allowed because it is not an absolute restriction on your neighbor's ownership of the car.

Pets are more than animals, they are family members. Therefore, it is only natural for people to want to leave their property to their pets. However, you cannot leave money or property to a pet because, in the eyes of the law, an animal cannot own property. There are ways of working around that. For example, you can leave money or property to a family member or friend with the condition that it be used to take care of your pets. If you set up a trust with a named executor to distribute funds to take care of your pets, the law will allow you to do that.

States that allow trusts for pets: Alaska, Arizona, Arkansas, California, Colorado, Washington, D.C., Florida, Hawaii, Idaho, Illinois, Iowa, Kansas, Maine, Michigan, Missouri, Montana, Nebraska, Nevada, New Hampshire, New Jersey, New Mexico, New York, North Carolina, Oregon, Tennessee, Texas, Utah, Washington (State), Wisconsin, and Wyoming.

G. Effects of Marital Status on Your Will

Marital status can usually be defined as single, married, or divorced. However, if you are going through a transitional phase, such as a separation or a court sanctioned separation which is ongoing at the time of your death, your state's laws may probate your will as if you are married. This means that your surviving spouse will receive their legal share of your estate, regardless of what you have written in your will. Also, if your divorce is pending (has not been finalized by the courts), or you are going through an annulment at the time of death, your relationship with your spouse will be defined as "married" under the law and your property will be distributed according to the marriage laws of the state.

Another possibility is that your relationship may be defined, under the law, as a common law marriage. *Common law marriage* is the union between two people that has not been formalized using the normal methods as prescribed by law, but is created by agreement to marry followed by cohabitation. For the purposes of probating your will, the court will consider you married if you are in a common law marriage in a state that recognizes common law marriages. Common law marriages are only recognized in certain states.

Note: to end a common law marriage, a spouse must formally file papers of a normal divorce. There is no separate divorce process for common law marriages. You cannot get out of a common law marriage simply by ending the cohabitation.

Common law marriages are recognized in: Alabama, Colorado, Washington, D.C., Georgia (only if created prior to January 1, 1997), Idaho (only if created prior to January 1, 1996), Iowa, Kansas, Montana, New Hampshire (only for inheritances), Ohio (only if created prior to October 10, 1991), Oklahoma, Pennsylvania (only if created prior to January 1, 2005), Rhode Island, South Carolina, Texas, and Utah.

H. How to Change an Existing Will

For most people, writing a will is not a one-time event. You should review your will periodically and consider whether you need to make any changes to reflect any new property that you have acquired. Also, reviewing your will can give you a chance to make changes if your wishes have changed. In addition, you should update your will following certain events, such as:

- a change in your marital status, such as if you get married, divorced, or remarried,
- the birth and/or adoption of children, from current or previous marriage(s), and/or grandchildren,
- the death of a parent, spouse, child, or anyone named in the will,
- if you make the decision to take someone out of your will,
- significant financial losses, gains, or if you incur any new debts,
- if you change your state of residence, or
- if you buy property in another state.

You can change your will after it has been signed and witnessed. There are several ways to make the changes, but the easiest way is to create a new will. In the new will, include a statement that all prior wills are superseded by this new will. Another way to make changes to your will is to create a *codicil*. A codicil is a separate document containing a statement of the changes to your will. A codicil can be used to change a single part of the will or multiple parts. With modern technology, it is easy to create a new will or create a codicil.

Failure to change your will can have unintended consequences. For example, if all of the people in your will are now dead, then your property will be distributed according to state law, which usually means the property will go to your relatives, and your wishes may not be fulfilled. If you have children after your will is created and your children are not named in your will because it has not been changed, then the court will decide who will care for your children. Keep in mind that any matters you do not address in your will may have to be addressed by your survivors who will incur the costs of litigating these matters, at their expense.

I.   Handwritten Wills

Remember there is no requirement that your will be typed. One option is to handwrite your will, called a *holographic will*. Witnesses are not required to be valid in most jurisdictions, but your holographic will must:

- be completely in your own handwriting (partially in your handwriting and partially in another's handwriting or typed with your initials above are generally not accepted),
- be signed and dated by you, and
- include a clear statement that it is your intention to make this your will.

Also remember that holographic wills are greatly disfavored by the courts and you should only create one if it is your only option. If it is possible to create a typed will, it is best that you do so.

J.   Simultaneous Death

Simultaneous death is a rare occurrence. *Simultaneous death* is the legal term for when both spouses die within a very short period from one another. A minority of states follow the rule that, if one spouse outlives the other, even by a few minutes or seconds, the last in time to survive will have their will govern the estate of both spouses. This can be problematic if it's hard to determine which spouse died last.

To alleviate this problem, many states have enacted a *Uniform Simultaneous Death Act*, which alleviates the problem of having to determine which spouse died last in time, so long as both spouses die within the specified amount of time set out by state law. Where both spouses die within the specified amount

of time from one another, the law considers each to have predeceased (died before) the other i.e., each spouse is considered to have died before the other spouse. All the property of one spouse will pass to the other spouse.

For example, New York's simultaneous death statute defines simultaneous death as one spouse dying within 72 hours of the other spouse. What that means is that, for will purposes, if one spouse dies within 72 hours of the other spouse, and New York law governs the estate, then all the property of the first spouse will be legally owned by the second spouse at the time of death.

Simultaneous deaths become an issue when the husband names his wife as his sole beneficiary and the wife names the husband as her sole beneficiary. In that case, each is said to have died before the other. In this case, both estates are divided up by a probate judge and the property distributed among the beneficiaries.

One way to avoid your state's simultaneous death statute is to include a survivorship provision in your will. A *survivorship provision* is a statement in your will stating one spouse must survive the other for a specified period of time (30-days is the default in the wills in this book) before the property of the deceased spouse can pass to the other spouse. Since you can make the time greater than the simultaneous death statute time period, you can avoid this unintended consequence of your named beneficiaries not inheriting your property. The time period must be a limited and reasonable period of time. Therefore, even if the husband and wife die "simultaneously" under the statute, the husband would not take the wife's property because of the survivorship requirement in her will and the property would pass to the wife's beneficiaries.

If both husband and wife include a survivorship provision in their will, and die simultaneously, then the court will make a determination as what to do according to state law and the facts of the situation. It is better to have a survivorship provision in your will so you have the best chance of having your wishes honored.

It is worth noting, again, that simultaneous deaths are rare occurrences.

K. Dying Without a Will

When a person dies without a will, they are referred to as having died *intestate*. If you do not create a will, the court will appoint a special representative who will distribute your property according to the laws of the state.

It's important to note that any property you own, but which is not included in your will is distributed by the special representative.

L. Taxes

Taxes are an important consideration. Only really large estates have complex tax returns to file, but other estates will likely need to file taxes with the Federal and state governments. There are ways to reduce your tax burden, but not many, if any, ways to avoid taxes all together. There is generally a tax payer. All estates should file taxes and be paid before any property is distributed. If your estate is

below the minimum amount required to file taxes, it is still advisable to file taxes so the government can take you off of their tax rolls. Filing taxes lets the government know that you have died and filing taxes is a good way to be checked off their list and avoid estate problems.

The money to pay taxes comes from your property, unless you have a surviving spouse who will be liable for taxes that are due. Even after you die, your estate may continue to generate income or losses from bank accounts and other investments. These gains and losses need to be reported to the government.

After you die, your executor (referred to by the IRS as a personal representative) must file a personal income tax return for the year that you died (January 1st until your death). Also, anyone that receives property from your estate, including a trustee and beneficiaries, will need to report the gains on their income taxes.

Both Federal and state governments tax an estate, but in different ways. State taxes can vary greatly between jurisdictions.

a) Federal Taxes

There are three possible Federal tax returns that need to be filed by your estate (all three may not be required):

- **Final income tax return**, (also referred to as the *individual income tax return*), IRS Form 1040, is required only if the deceased person earned more than the minimum amount of income in the year of death. As of the date of this book, that amount is income greater than $9,750 for a single person under 65 years of age, $11,200 for persons over 65 years of age, and $19,500 for married couples filing jointly plus $1,150 for each spouse aged 65 or older. It is due April 15 of the year following death.

- **Trust income tax return**, IRS Form 1041, is required if there is a trust and the trust receives more than a minimum amount of income. As of the date of this book, that amount is income $600 or greater. This tax return is not required if the minimum income is not met or you're the surviving spouse and inherited your spouse's property through a trust that leaves everything to you in a revocable living trust (you will report income gains or losses from the assets on your individual tax returns). It is due April 15 of the year following death, but in some cases, you can choose a different reporting period.

- **Estate tax return**, IRS Form 706, is required if the person died with more than the amount excluded from estate tax. This is required only for very large estates. As of the date of this book, that amount is greater than $5.12 million of taxable income. It is due nine months following death.

In addition to taxes on your estate, there might be penalties. IRS penalties can add up quickly. First, failure to file a return incurs a penalty of 5% of the tax due for each month a return is late, up to a maximum of 25%. Also, failure to pay the tax is penalized at 0.5% for each month the tax isn't paid. This has no maximum cap.

b) State Taxes

In addition to Federal taxes, state taxes may also need to be paid by your estate. If your estate has any state taxes that are due, the executor will need to file the state tax return and pay the tax before making distributions. The possible state tax returns include:

- **Final state income tax return** which is required if the deceased person earned more than a minimal amount of income in the year of death, as determined by the state. It is due April 15 of the year following death.

- **State trust income tax return** which is required if there is a trust and the trust receives more than a minimum amount of income. The due date will depend on state law.

- **State estate tax return** which is required if the estate is large enough. The amount varies between $675,000 and $3.5 million, depending on state law. The due date will also depend on state law. States with estate taxes are: Connecticut, Delaware, Hawaii, Illinois, Maine, Maryland, Massachusetts, Minnesota, New Jersey, New York, North Carolina (repealed for deaths as of January 1, 2013), Ohio (repealed for deaths as of January 1, 2013), Oregon, Rhode Island, Tennessee (repealed for deaths as of January 1, 2013), Vermont, Washington (State), and Washington, D.C.

- **State inheritance tax return** which is required if the state imposes it. The due date will depend on state law. The inheritance tax is dependent on the relationship of the beneficiary to the deceased. Spouses are always exempt from inheritance tax. Other beneficiaries pay depending on how close they were to the deceased person. There may be one tax rate for lineal descendants (e.g., children, grandchildren) and another rate for everyone else. Inheritance tax is imposed by the deceased person's state regardless of where the new owner lives. States with inheritance taxes include: Indiana (20%), Iowa (15%), Kentucky (16%), Maryland (10%), Nebraska (18%), New Jersey (16%), Pennsylvania (15%), and Tennessee (9.5%).

M. Probate Court

Probate court is a court that handles primarily estate administration such as validating a will, distributing property, and naming guardians if required. Your will must be filed in probate court by your executor or a family member. The court will determine if your will is valid, then your property will be collected by the executor you chose, and then the court will distribute your property after all debts and taxes have been paid. This determination by the court is known as *probate*. A will is not legally binding until it goes through probate. The exact process of probating a will can vary greatly from court to court. It can only take place after your death. Probate is sometimes called *estate administration*.

a) What Property Goes Through Probate?

In probate there are two types of property; probate property and non-probate property.

Probate property is property that you own at the time of your death that is specifically named to beneficiaries in your will. If your will does not mention a property that you own at the time of your death or you have not created a will, then your property will be distributed according to state law.

Non-probate property is property that you do not own at the time of your death, and is, therefore, not subject to probate. Examples of non-probate property include life insurance (on your life) payable to beneficiaries, a trust (containing your property) with named beneficiaries, or any joint property you own with rights of survivorship.

Although the categories may seem elementary, categorizing your property before you make your will makes it easier to identify what property is not part of your will. A will does not control non-probate property. Naming non-probate property in your will has no effect on the property. Therefore, if you do name non-probate property in your will, it will not pass according to your will. While probate property is required to be distributed through probate court, non-probate does not. The named beneficiary of non-probate property can get the property distributed to them by proving to the person or organization that is in possession of the property that you have died.

b) How to Avoid Probate Court

There are many ways to avoid your property having to go through probate court. Some of them are discussed throughout the book. Although not a complete list, ways of avoiding probate that are discussed in this book are:

- *joint tenancy with right of survivorship*— property owned by two or more people with the understanding that the last one of them to live will take all of the property, and the others (who die before any of the others) take nothing,
- *community property*—in a community property state, each spouse brings into the marriage one-half of all property acquired by either spouse during the marriage,
- *pay on death accounts*—an account (often bank accounts, securities, real estate deeds, and car registration) that passes to a designated beneficiary upon the death of the owner,
- life insurance,
- retirement accounts,
- trusts, and
- you can give your property away as gifts during your lifetime.

N. Next Steps to Creating Your Will

Now that you have a basic understanding of what a will is and how creating a will can be beneficial for you, the next step is to understand who can receive your property upon your death. Not everyone is the same under the eyes of the law. A person's relationship to you, may determine how much of your property they must inherit. After you identify the person you would like to leave property to, you can identify the property you wish to leave them.

3. Identifying the People in Your Will

Once you understand the basic functions of a will, your next step is to understand how someone can be named in your will. Certain people, because of their special relationship to you, must be named in your will. In this chapter, you will learn about the different people who you can give your property to in your will.

A. People in Your Will are Beneficiaries

Any person or organization that you name in your will, or is included under the terms of documents such as insurance policies or retirement accounts, is called a *beneficiary*. If you do not have a will, the law dictates that certain members of your family inherit your property. Family members who inherit your property are called *heirs*.

The four main categories of beneficiaries that you should be aware of are:

a) primary beneficiaries,
b) alternate beneficiaries,
c) residuary beneficiaries, and
d) alternate residuary beneficiaries.

Certain states require that you mention your spouse and children in your will, even if you do not leave them anything, as a way of showing that you were of "sound mind" when you created the will.

a) Primary Beneficiaries

A *primary beneficiary* is the person you choose to receive property. If they are named in your will, then you have chosen them to receive property. You can have one primary beneficiary who will receive all of your property, or you can have multiple primary beneficiaries. If you want to give different people or organizations different things, once you name them in your will, they are all primary beneficiaries. You do not have to leave them equal shares of your property. All primary beneficiary must be specifically mentioned in your will along with the property you want them to receive. If they are not mentioned, they are not a primary beneficiary.

You can name multiple people and instruct them to share a single property. See below for considerations in naming shared beneficiaries. As a general rule, naming percentages of property is favored over using dollar amounts. This helps avoid the consequences of fluctuations in prices where inflation can play a part in property value that is not in cash form. If you use dollar amounts, and the property value falls below the amount that you have specified, the court may seek to satisfy the dollar amount by supplementing from elsewhere in the estate which can have the unintended consequence of giving a lesser share of your estate to another beneficiary. A percentage, on the other hand, will remain relative to the value. So, even if the value drops, the percentage will not change. Make sure that if you do split your property into percentages, that the sum of all the percentages equals 100%.

b) Alternate Beneficiaries

Just as the primary beneficiary is your first choice to receive property when you die, the *alternate beneficiary* is the person or organization you choose to act as an alternative to receive your property in the event that the primary beneficiary dies prior to your death or does not want the property. The alternate beneficiary is your second choice. Naming an alternate beneficiary is not required, but many people choose to name one because it's good planning. Also, naming an alternate beneficiary keeps you from having to make another will if a primary beneficiary dies before you do.

You can name property to be shared between two or more people. You can name alternate beneficiaries to any of those receiving shared property. For example, if the property is a rare book and 50% ownership is left to friend A, by name, and the other 50% is left to friend B, by name, you can still name an alternative to friend A or to friend B. If a beneficiary has predeceased you and you don't name an alternative beneficiary, the property will pass by state law. It may go to the other friend, to a family member, or to the residuary beneficiary. The *residuary beneficiary* is the beneficiary who receives any remaining property of the estate that you owned at the time of death not left to anyone else in the will or otherwise.

The alternate beneficiary does not have to be a person; it can be an organization. Note that naming a human, primary beneficiary does not mean that you cannot name an organization as an alternate beneficiary, or vice versa. You are free to select any combination you want. The alternate beneficiary must be named as an alternate beneficiary in your will along with the property to be transferred.

You can also name an alternate beneficiary for the alternate beneficiary. For example, you can leave your house to friend A, in the event of A's death, the house goes to B, in the event of B's death the house goes to C. You can name as many alternate beneficiaries as you want. Naming multiple, alternate beneficiaries is uncommon because naming a primary and an alternate is usually enough, and the residuary beneficiary will take the remainder of the property if the primary and alternate are not available. One additional alternate may be reasonable under certain circumstances. In general, though, you only need to name one alternate for each major piece of property you own, such as a house.

When you name an alternate beneficiary, you can specify the period of time the alternate beneficiary must live before they can take ownership of the property. The period is known as a *survivorship period*. This period is filled in as 30 days in the sample wills in this book but, that number is not required and the amount of days can be changed. (See also simultaneous death.)

For example, if you use the sample wills in this book, then you can name your best friend as your primary beneficiary with a 30 day survivorship period and a different friend as your alternate beneficiary. So, if you die on January 1, and the primary beneficiary lives past January 31, then the primary beneficiary will inherit. But, if your primary beneficiary dies on January 15, then they will not have lived past the 30 day survivorship period and so your alternate beneficiary will inherit. Why can survivorship periods be important? If you die on January 1 and then your primary beneficiary dies on January 15, and you have not written a survivorship period clause, then your property would go to your primary beneficiary who has died and then the property will pass according to their will, bypassing your wishes.

c)   Residuary Beneficiaries

The *residuary beneficiary* is the person or organization who inherits the remainder of your estate that you do not mention in your will or give away elsewhere. The reason a residual beneficiary exists in the law, is because it is very difficult to name everything that you own. The residuary beneficiary is named in your will, but no property needs to be described. Anything left over after all specific property has been distributed (to the primary and/or alternate beneficiaries) will go to the residuary beneficiary.

You can name more than one residuary beneficiary by saying, for example, that you want 50% of the residuary estate to go to your son, residuary 1, and the other 50% to your daughter, residuary 2. See below section *Naming Shared Beneficiaries*.

d)   Alternate Residuary Beneficiaries

Just like the alternate beneficiary, the *alternate residuary beneficiary* takes the place of the residuary beneficiary if the residuary beneficiary dies before you. Naming an alternative residuary beneficiary is not required, but, if you want to name one, you must do so by using specific language. You can also name a survivorship period for the alternate residuary beneficiaries.

B.   Charitable Organizations and the Government as Beneficiaries

Many people choose to name charitable organizations as beneficiaries. Charitable organizations include nonprofits as well as houses of worships, e.g. the American Red Cross, your local food bank, temples, and churches. However, there are certain limitations you should keep in mind when you name one of these organizations as a beneficiary in your will.

If you choose to leave a large amount of money to a charitable organization, many states place a time limit prior to death, when you are not allowed to change your will to exclude the charity. The states created these time limits in order to notify the charity that they will not receive the large sum that they may have depended on and to give that charity time to look for funding elsewhere to make up for the amount of money you are no longer giving them. Your state rules will govern exactly what you can do. If a charity is relying on your future gift, the money or property you left to that charity in your will, and you change your will without telling that charity, the charity may be able to successfully sue your estate for that money after you die. And so, to prevent these kinds of confusions and lawsuits, it is important that you carefully consider what charity/charities you want to name in your will and how much you want to leave to them.

Most states place a limit on how much of your estate you can give to charity; the limit is usually around 50%. The reason certain states have such a limit is to prevent people from giving away all of their property in the hopes that they will be forgiven for past conduct at the expense of taking from their heirs.

Some people want to leave money to the government that is not in the form of taxes. You are allowed to do that. You can leave money to the United States and that money will go to the Federal government. You can also specifically leave money to a state or local government.

C. Naming Shared Beneficiaries

The biggest concern you should have when naming a shared beneficiary is the potential conflicts that come with shared ownership. The wills in this book assume that all shared gifts will be sold with the proceeds split according to the will, unless all of the

beneficiaries agree in writing that the property does not need to be sold.

It can be difficult for multiple beneficiaries to share the same property. This is especially true when the property is something like a house where the property cannot be divided into pieces. If you choose to leave a single piece of property, like a house, to multiple beneficiaries, it is helpful to also describe the percentage of the property that each beneficiary will own.

If you name multiple beneficiaries, but do not mention their share of ownership, the court will assume each is to get an equal share. If you do name a relative share to the beneficiaries, you can name disproportionate shares. For example you can give 25% ownership to one beneficiary and 75% to the other. If you do not want your will to operate this way, you should seek resources outside of this book.

D. Who Cannot Be a Beneficiary

There are certain people who cannot inherit as a beneficiary, even if they are expressly named in your will. These people are disqualified from being beneficiaries in your will. If a disqualified beneficiary is named in your will the court will not honor your wishes regarding the distribution to the disqualified beneficiary and the property will pass to the next person eligible to inherit as set out in your will or by state law.

The following are disqualified beneficiaries:

- anyone involved in creating the will,

  - including the attorney who drafted your will because it would be assumed that the attorney participated only so they would be included in your will.
  - generally, states do not allow anyone who serves as a witness to your will to be named as a beneficiary. It is much safer to not have any beneficiaries act as witnesses.

- anyone who murders you,

  - this just makes practical sense. If someone named in your will kills you, then the killer, and anyone who participates in your killing, is disqualified from being your beneficiary.

- generally, states do not allow unincorporated associations to be named as a beneficiary in your will,

  - an *unincorporated association* is a general partnership that is not registered with the state but is acting as a business entity.

- any for-profit corporations,

- animals (but remember that you can leave money in a trust to pay for the care of your animals), or

- minors.

  - either the court will appoint a guardian or you can appoint someone to manage the property until they are legally an adult.
  - minors require adult supervision to inherit property. You can appoint a specific person to manage the property until the minor reaches the age of majority. If you do not appoint an adult supervisor, the court will appoint a guardian.

E. Disinheriting Spouses, Children, and Others

Disinheriting someone means that you want to keep them from getting your property when you die. People that you want to disinherit fall into three categories: spouses, children, or others.

Spouses are difficult to disinherit. In most states, you are not allowed to disinherit a spouse. If you are married at the time of death, then by law, your spouse is entitled to receive a certain portion of your estate. Until a divorce has been finalized, you must account for the surviving spouse's shares or the court will take property in your estate given to other beneficiaries to satisfy the spouses share.

If you are divorced at the time of your death then most states do not require that you leave anything to the surviving divorced spouse. States are for the most part, common law states, meaning that you cannot legally disinherit a spouse that has not been divorced at the time of marriage. The other states are community property states, meaning that most of the property that is acquired during the marriage is owned together by each of the spouses. In both common law states and community property states, if you are married at the time of your death, then you should leave one-half of your estate to the surviving spouse. If you fail to do so, then the spouse might be able to get more than half from your estate, depending on how the court rules.

Children can be disinherited, but you must do so with specific language. Just failing to mention your children will not be enough to disinherit them. But, if you leave your child a very small amount, such as one dollar, that child will be considered disinherited. Minor children cannot be disinherited, but those over 18 can be disinherited with specific language.

Others can be easily disinherited by not naming them in the will. That would include your siblings, parents, grandchildren, and friends. There is no need to leave one dollar because they are not entitled to anything if they are not mentioned.

F. What Happens If the Beneficiary Rejects the Property?

It's very rare that someone rejects an inheritance, so rare that most people don't think about it because, generally, no one rejects property given in a will. Acceptance of an inheritance is assumed, unless action is taken to reject the gift in the will. A beneficiary can reject an inheritance by informing the executor or the court appointed special representative of their desire not to receive the property.

There are a few reasons why a beneficiary might not want the property. For example, a person may reject property to avoid negative tax consequences. Some people don't want the hassle of dealing with out of state property.

Whatever the reason, a beneficiary has the right to reject property by stating their rejection clearly at the time the will is probated.

When a named beneficiary rejects property, the property passes to the alternate beneficiary, the residuary, the alternate residuary beneficiary, and then according to state law.

G. Guardians for Minor Child(ren)

A *personal guardian* is, by definition, someone other than a legal parent who will be responsible for raising minor child(ren) in the event that the legal parents die. A personal guardian cannot take the place of a living legal parent, but only takes care of the child(ren) should both of the parents die. Courts are generally very reluctant to separate a child from their parents, especially following the death of one of the parents.

When deciding who to name as a personal guardian for your child(ren) in your will, remember that the person you name could be raising your child(ren). The personal guardian must be an adult of at least 18 years of age. You should consider how likely it is that the person you name will accept the responsibility and whether or not you can trust that person to act in the best interest of child(ren). The personal guardian you name in your will does not have to accept the responsibility and is not bound until they agree in court and a judge appoints them as the legal guardian of the minor child(ren). Along with naming a personal guardian, it is common to name an alternate guardian in your will.

When you name a personal guardian for your child(ren), you should include a clause in your will stating your reasons for naming that person. You should also include a similar clause for why you chose the alternate guardian. These clauses can help the court in a situation where there is conflict about who should get the child(ren).

It is important that both parents name the same personal guardians and alternate personal guardians to avoid conflicts about who will take care of the minor child(ren) in the case of simultaneous death.

Custody requests in your will are not automatically honored. A judge will make the final determination as to what is in the best interests of your minor child(ren).

Sometimes you may need to name different personal guardians for your child(ren), i.e. split up the child(ren). This is only done in extremely rare cases, but it can be done with a clause that specifically states your intention to name separate personal guardians for each child. It is helpful to describe the reasons why you believe it is in the best interest of the child(ren) to have different personal guardians.

You do not need to appoint a personal guardian for any child(ren) who have reached 18 years of age. If you have a child who requires special care, such as a special needs child, please seek additional resources from a lawyer on ways to ensure they get the best care.

H. Witnesses

Two witnesses are required for a will to be valid in every state, except for Vermont which requires three witnesses. The legal requirement for witnesses is often overlooked by those creating a will, but without witnesses a will cannot be enforceable. There is no requirement that you know the witnesses.

The rules about witnesses are different in every state. For example, there are some states that allow a witness to a will to be under the age of 18 and some states allow a witness to be a beneficiary. While following the laws in your state is recommended, the trend in the law, in all states is to require a witness to be a non-beneficiary who is over the age of 18. To avoid the risk of a change in law, it's advisable that all witnesses to your will be non-beneficiaries who are over the age of 18.

I. Executor

The *executor* (also referred to as *personal representative*) is the person that you choose to complete the "winding up" of your estate, according to your will. The executor will take charge of your property through the probate process, or other means, and distribute your property according to your will. The entire process usually takes around six months to two years to complete, depending on the specifics of your situation and applicable state laws. If you do not name an executor, or the executor and the alternate executor that you name die before you, the court will appoint an administrator.

The executor is entitled to be paid for their services. State laws will generally suggest a standard of reasonable compensation, the amount of which will be dependent upon how much work the executor is expected to do on your estate's behalf. Your will is generally not expected to describe in hourly detail, the projected amount of work the executor will do, but, will usually state a lump sum or a percentage of the estate that will be the executor's compensation. However, it is not uncommon for an executor to accept no compensation and simply take on the responsibility out of love, or as a last gesture of kindness.

You can name anyone to be your executor, including beneficiaries. In fact, most people name a spouse or adult child who is going to get the majority of the property as the executor. This is perfectly legal. Be careful to consider whether your choice in executor will cause or enflame any familial conflicts. Instead of a family member, you can choose to name a friend or other third party, such as a lawyer, CPA, bank, or a trust to act as your beneficiary. Remember that certain professionals will need to be compensated for their services.

Prior to naming your executor and alternate executor in your will, you should discuss your decision with the people you want to choose and decide whether they are likely to act responsibly. Trust is the key. You don't want to name an executor that won't fulfill their duties, or worse. It is best to have a candid conversation with your potential executor(s) about your expectations and how you want your property to be distributed.

The executor is not required to keep any beneficiary informed about what the executor does in relation to the property in the estate, i.e. the executor can take whatever action the executor thinks is appropriate without having to consult or even inform beneficiaries before or after the actions occur. While there are limited legal actions your beneficiaries can take if your executor does not listen to the beneficiaries, as long as the actions of the beneficiary are reasonable, the executor is left to do their job. For the most part, the executor is given broad discretion to do the executor's job in a competent manner.

Naming co-executors is beyond the scope of this book because of the multitude of state specific, special rules relating to co-executors. For example, there might be a requirement that the co-executors agree before they can take any action which can make the process longer, and potentially more frustrating, if there is a fundamental disagreement.

You should name an executor and an alternate executor in your will. The duties of the executor will likely include:

- **Gathering the property of the testator and prepare an inventory.** This means getting all of the paperwork in order, collecting items that would be in danger of falling into disrepair such as a car, and monitoring bank accounts and investments.

- **Taking care of the property until it is time to hand it over to the beneficiaries.** This means that the executor will be responsible for any upkeep of your property and taking care of the house until it is time to distribute it. It does not mean that the executor has to perform physical labor, only that the executor will do what is in the best interest of the property to ensure the property is not damaged before it is distributed to your beneficiaries. Any executor acting in the best interest of the property may hire a gardener, make financial decisions, or decisions related to any businesses that are named in the will. These expenses are paid out of the estate's property before distribution to beneficiaries.

- **Selling any property that needs to be sold.** You can choose to instruct the executor of your will to sell your property and distribute the proceeds to your beneficiaries. If you choose for the executor to sell your property, they will be responsible for finding buyers and getting fair market value for the property. Note that certain states require the executors to get prior approval from the court before selling real estate.

- **Hiring attorneys and other professionals.** Where the estate requires a skill set that is beyond the scope of the executor's skill set or expertise, and the estate would likely benefit from the services of a professional, the executor is responsible for hiring and paying professionals. For example, if it is a large estate and the executor reasonably believes the estate would benefit from a tax attorney or accountant, then the executor can retain professional services which are paid from estate property.

- **Paying debts and taxes.** All property that is transferred by your will must be transferred after having paid any debts and taxes owed on that property. The executor is not personally liable for any debts and taxes, but the executor is responsible for filing the applicable paperwork on your estate's behalf. Generally, this means paying one year's taxes.

- Note: You cannot inherit someone else's debt. A person's property will be sold to pay off their debts: first, funeral and probate court costs, second, whatever funds are left, if any, will be used to pay off any remaining debts attached to the estate. If the remaining funds are not enough to cover the estate's outstanding debts, and there is no more property in the estate, then the creditors are out of luck and cannot come after the beneficiaries. In some states, the creditors must go through probate to force the sale of property to collect on a debt. If the testator has distributed their property in a way that eliminates the need for probate, then the creditors cannot gain access to that property. If there is no property to sell to settle the testator's debts, those debts will be wiped out.

- **Paying off secured debts may not be required.** Debts secured by property, such as a mortgage or vehicle loan, are called *secured debts* or *liens*. Generally, secured debts do not have to be paid off before the property is distributed because banks may allow the beneficiary to take over your loan, but it is the bank's decision. If the bank does not transfer over the loan to your beneficiary, then the beneficiary has the option to pay off the debt with the money the beneficiary has personally, can apply for a new loan with their credit secured by the house, or allow the bank to sell the property and collect the balance after the loan and fees are paid. Banks rarely exercise this power and allow the new owner to continue under the existing loan. If you want your estate to pay off the secured debts before transferring to the beneficiary, you need to state your wishes in your will.

- **Distributing the property when it is time to do so.** The distribution of the testator's property will occur after probate. If the property is non-probate property, the executor can distribute that property immediately or in a reasonable amount of time.

- **Distributing the remaining property according to the will or by state law.** Once the will has been settled and/or probated, and the property is distributed to the beneficiaries, any property not distributed will be given to the named residuary beneficiary or distributed according to state law.

To guarantee that the executor will not waste the money and property in the estate, you may want to require that your executor post a bond. Where a will states that a bond is not required, a court, generally, will not require one. If your will does not state a bond requirement, the court may require the executor to post a bond before the court will approve the will. If the executor is an out of state resident, the court may impose a bond regardless of what is in the will. Bonds are not required for any executor of the wills in this book.

Out of state executors are often not allowed by state law in order for the state to ensure it keeps jurisdiction over the executor. The executor has broad control over the estate. By requiring an in-state executor, the courts have jurisdiction over the executor which may prevent dishonesty on behalf of the executor. For that reason, most states will not allow an out of state executor. Even where allowed, naming an out of state executor can have some unintended restrictions:

- **Alabama.** Out of state residents can serve as executors in Alabama only if the property in Alabama is part of an estate which includes property located in the executor's estate.

- **Florida.** Out of state residents can only serve as executors in Florida only if they are legally related to the testator by blood or marriage.

- **Iowa.** Out of state residents can serve as executors in Iowa only if there is named a co-executors who is a residents of Iowa, or where the court approves the out of state executors to serve alone.

- **Kentucky.** Out of state residents can only serve as executors in Kentucky only if they are legally related to the testator by blood or marriage.

- **Nevada.** Out of state residents can serve as executors in Nevada only if there is named a co-executors who is a resident of Nevada.

- **Ohio.** Out of state residents can only serve as executors in Ohio only if they are legally related to the testator by blood or marriage or the out of state residents is from a state that allows out of state residents to serve as executors.

- **Pennsylvania.** Out of state residents can only serve as executors after getting permission from the register of wills which the executor gets by filing out an affidavit stating that the deceased has no debt in Pennsylvania, and that the executor will not engage in any conduct that is prohibited in the executor's state of residence.

- **Tennessee.** Out of state residents can only serve as executors in Tennessee if they are legally related to the testator or only if there is named a co-executor who is a resident of Tennessee.

- **Vermont.** Out of state residents can only serve as executors in Vermont if the court approves a request for approval made by the surviving spouse, adult children, or the parents or legal guardians of minor children.

J. Next Steps to Creating Your Will

Now that you have an idea about how people can receive your property and how to classify those people in your will, the next chapter will teach you how to identify and classify the property that you will leave to people in your will.

4. Identifying the Property in Your Will

After you have identified the people you would like to include in your will, the next natural thing to do is to identify the property you would like to leave those people in your will. Understanding how your property is owned is the key to classifying your property. Classifying your property will help you decide how to distribute the property in your will. In this chapter, you will identify how property is owned and then learn how you want your property distributed in your will.

A. What Property Can Be Distributed by Will?

You can leave any property that you own, at the time of your death, to someone in your will. If you no longer own the property because you sold it or have given it away, then it cannot be distributed in your will and the provision granting that property is void. So, if you decide to give away or sell a piece of property that you had previously named in your will the person you sold or gave your property to gets to keep it.

You are allowed to make specific gifts in your will. Giving someone a specific gift in your will is called a *specific bequest*. For example, you can will to your niece a specific, blue mirror.

The laws of the state of your permanent residence will, generally, apply to the property distributed according to your will. If the property distributed in your will is real estate in another state or country, the laws of the state or country where the real estate property sits will govern.

B. What Property Cannot Be Distributed by Will?

Property in a trust. Property that is in a trust, including in a living trust, cannot be left in a will.

Accounts you've already named beneficiaries for. Insurance policies, retirement accounts, pension plans, and pay on death accounts in which you have already named beneficiaries cannot be distributed by will because the property is automatically distributed upon your death.

Shares of a business that you own. If you own transferable or inheritable shares of a business, then those shares, or income from those shares, can be left to a person in your will, but only to the extent that you own those shares and no more.

Joint tenancy property. An entirely separate category of property that cannot be distributed by will is property that is owned with another person in a joint tenancy with rights of survivorship. See next section, *How Can Property Be Owned*.

Money to animals. Any will provision that leaves property outright to an animal will not be followed because animals cannot own property.

C. How Can Property Be Owned?

Identifying and understanding how property is owned will help you determine how your property can be distributed in your will, if at all. In this section, you will learn about solely owned property, the different ways in which property can be jointly owned, and about the special rules that govern property that is acquired during a marriage.

a) Solely Owned Property

Solely owned property that you own by yourself, separate from even your spouse is the easiest to leave in your will. If the property is solely owned by you, then you can name the property in your will as a specific bequest. This is true regardless of whether there is any debt attached to it (such as a lien). If you do owe any debt on the property, the debt will need to be paid before the property passes because you cannot, generally, inherit another person's debts. But debts protected by a lien, such as a house mortgage or car loan, are called *secured debts*, and, generally, do not have to be paid off before the property is distributed. Although a bank legally has the final call if the secured debt is to be paid in full following the death of the secured debt owner. Banks rarely exercise this right and allow transfers of secured debts. If there is a default, then the bank can take the property.

b) Jointly Held Property

Jointly held property can present some unique challenges when you are trying to transfer the property in your will. Mainly, it presents a problem because you are not the sole owner and the rights of the other joint holder in the property should be considered.

States have three ways property can be jointly owned:

1) Tenancy in common,
2) Joint tenancy with right of survivorship, and
3) Tenancy by the entirety.

i. Tenancy in Common

Tenancy in common is a term used to describe a type of ownership of property where a property is owned, jointly, with all of the joint holders of the property having a right to the use and enjoyment of the entire property, not just a portion of the land. However, each owner owns a percentage of the property that can be freely transferred, without approval from the other owners. In other words, you own the right to use all of the property in any way you choose, and you can sell your share without having to notify the other owners.

Where parties try to create a joint tenancy with rights of survivorship, but fail to do so, usually because of a failure to comply with legal formalities, a tenancy in common will be created. The tenancy in common is used by the courts as a default because judges favor the free transfer of property that the tenancy in common offers. See below *Joint Tenancy with Rights of Survivorship* section for more details.

If your state recognizes tenancy by the entirety for married couples, then spouses can own property together. See below *Tenancy by the Entirety* section for more details.

ii. Joint Tenancy with Rights of Survivorship

Property that is owed as *joint tenancy with rights of survivorship*, the property is owned by two or more people with the understanding that the last one of them to live owns all of the property. Where a joint tenancy with rights of survivorship is created, all *joint tenants*, the owners with the rights of survivorship, have a right to the use and enjoyment of the entire property. For example, Greenacre is owned by A, B, and C as joint tenants with rights of survivorship. Each owns one-third of Greenacre. C dies. Now, A owns one-half and B owns one-half. C's heirs have no interest in Greenacre. Now, B dies. A owns Greenacre. B and C's heirs have no interest in Greenacre.

Joint tenants can transfer their interest in the property by selling it. When one joint tenant sells their interest in a property, the new owner becomes a tenant in common with no rights of survivorship. For example, Blackacre is owned by A, B, and C as joint tenants with rights of survivorship. Each owns one-third of Blackacre. C sell's their interest to D. A and B still own one-third interest each in Blackacre as joint tenants, but now the remaining one-third share is owned by D as a tenant in common. That is because when C sold to D, C broke the joint tenancy and

created a tenancy in common. Now, if C dies, D is still one-third owner as a tenant in common and, A and B remain joint tenants with rights of survivorship of the other two-third interest. C has no interest in Blackacre. Now, B dies. A owns two-thirds of Blackacre as a tenant in common with D, who owns the remaining one-third interest.

If, in the rare event, both joint tenants die simultaneously, each will be presumed to have predeceased the other and neither will take under a claim of survivorship. Both deceased will be treated as if they own one-third of the property and their shares will pass according to their will.

It is important to note that a joint tenancy with rights of survivorship is not favored by courts because it restricts the free transfer of property. So, to create a joint tenancy, you must use specific language by naming each joint tenant with their relative shares, and saying that you are all creating a "joint tenancy with the rights of survivorship." Check your state's rules as they may differ on the specific language required to create a joint tenancy. If specific language is not used, then a tenancy in common is created and not a joint tenancy with rights of survivorship.

If you create a joint tenancy with a right of survivorship in your will for others, for example, to your three children, be mindful of the potential for familial conflict.

Alaska does not recognize the joint tenancy with rights of survivorship.

iii. Tenancy by the Entirety

The *tenancy by the entirety* is a type of joint tenancy with rights of survivorship, but it can only be created between married couples, with the use of specific language that states that both spouses are creating a "tenancy by the entirety." Otherwise a tenancy in common is created. Laws regarding tenancy by the entirety vary greatly by state.

The primary difference between the joint tenancy with rights of survivorship and the tenancy by the entirety is that, in a tenancy by the entirety, one spouse cannot transfer interest in the property without consent of the other spouse. Creditors cannot attach interest to, and sell, a property without consent to attach an interest from both spouses.

You can only extinguishing a tenancy by the entirety by divorce, annulment, or by a joint agreement to amend any title property. At the death of one spouse, the surviving spouse takes full ownership of the property owned by a tenancy by the entirety.

In a tenancy by the entirety, both spouses have the right to enjoy all of the property.

States that allow tenancy by the entirety: Alaska (only for real estate), Arkansas, Connecticut, Delaware, Washington, D.C., Florida, Hawaii, Illinois (only for real estate), Indiana (only for real estate), Kentucky (only for real estate), Maryland, Massachusetts, Michigan, Mississippi, Missouri, New Jersey, New York (only for real estate), North Carolina (only for real estate), Ohio (only for real estate and if created before 4/4/1985), Oklahoma, Oregon (only for real estate), Pennsylvania, Rhode Island, Tennessee, Utah, Vermont, Virginia, and Wyoming.

c) Special Considerations for Marital Property

It is common for a spouse to leave most or all of their property to their surviving spouse. The law does not interfere with this. So long as you are distributing at least one-half of your estate to your spouse, there are, generally, no legal implications.

i. How Can Marital Property Be Owned?

When you want to leave property to someone other than your surviving spouse, a judge will determine who the property belongs to, i.e. is the property yours to give away? This answer will depend on whether your state is a community property state or a common law property state.

Note that prenuptial agreements are valid contracts and may be binding on the couples who enter into them. If you entered into a prenuptial agreement with your spouse prior to your marriage, then the prenuptial agreement may dictate whether certain property is considered community property or not.

1. Community Property States

Community property states are Alaska (only by written agreement), Arizona, California, Idaho, Nevada, New Mexico, Texas, Washington (State), and Wisconsin (a hybrid State where marital property law closely resembles community property states and covers all property owned at the time of death).

In a *community property state*, most property acquired during the marriage is owned equally (50%) by each spouse. Generally, if the property is acquired during the marriage, then it is community property, regardless of which spouse acquired it. For example, community property is:

- wages from employment and income earned by either spouse,
- property purchased from community property,
- gifts given to both spouses (which would include wedding gifts), and
- separate property which can be converted into community property if the separate property is mixed with community property so that what is separate and what is community property cannot be distinguished, or separate property that is converted into community property when the owner of the separate property converts the property into community property.

In a community property state, property that is owned by one spouse is either:

- their one-half share of community property that is owned together with the other spouse, or
- *separate property* which is defined as property acquired:
    - before the marriage,
    - during the marriage, or
        - with your own private, separate funds,
        - property purchased with the income from any property owned prior to the marriage that is sold because that income will be separate property (except in Washington state where it is considered community property),
        - gifts or inheritances received during the marriage but named specifically only to one spouse, or
        - community property converted into separate property by gift or written agreement.
    - after the marriage reaches a legal end.

For the most part, identifying what is community property and what is separate property will not be difficult. The vast majority of your property is community property. Here are the major problem areas:

- **Debts:** Personal debt not owned by the other spouse, will remain that spouse's individual responsibility. However, if one person in the marriage goes into debt acquiring necessities, such as food and/or shelter, that debt will be defined as marital debt. Necessities are a special category of things that are absolutely essential for life which can include food, shelter, and/or clothing. Often, the line between personal and community debt can be unclear.

- **Businesses:** If the business was owned by one of the spouses prior to the marriage, but continued during the marriage, any increase in the value of the business will likely be community property, but whether the remaining property is community property is not always clear.

- **Pensions:** Generally, pensions are community property. However, some, for example, Social Security retirement benefits and some other Federal pensions, are not. It is important to check your individual pension plan.

Usually, upon your death, one-half of all community property belongs to your surviving spouse. In your will, you may name your half of the community property in any way you choose.

2. Common Law Property States

States that are not community property states are *common law property states*. In a common law property state, individual property is:

- property purchased using income from employment and income earned separately from the other spouse, and

- property you own in only your name, so long as the property has ownership documents such as a deed or title.

If you use your personal income to purchase a house, but put your name and your spouse's name on the title, then both of you will own the house. If your spouse uses their personal funds to purchase a house, but only puts your name on the house, then you, not your spouse, own the house.

When a piece of property does not have a legal document that gives title to a named person, the property belongs to the person whose income was used to purchase that property. If the funds used to purchase a piece of property are jointly owned, then the property purchased with those funds is jointly owned.

In a common law property state, *separate property* is property held in only one of the spouse's names, regardless of who paid for the property.

In a common law property state, marital property is defined as property jointly owned by both spouses. So long as both names are on the title, or some other formal legal document, both spouses own the property no matter how the property was acquired.

ii. Spousal Shares

In almost every state, the surviving spouse is entitled to a share of the deceased spouse's share of property. Where a will fails to account for the surviving spouse's share, the court will take from the other beneficiaries to ensure that the surviving spouse gets their share. The percentage that the court will take from the other beneficiaries is called *elective shares*. In most states, elective shares range from one-third to one-half of all property in the estate that goes through probate, but some states will also include property that avoids probate. Some states will also consider whether the property is marital property or separate property.

As a rule of thumb, to be safe, you should leave 50% of your estate to your surviving spouse. If you want to provide less than the spousal share required by your state, then you will need to consult with a lawyer because that is beyond the scope of this book.

iii. Avoiding Spousal Shares

Spousal shares can be decreased by reducing the amount courts consider marital property.

One way to reduce your spouse's spousal share is to use of a prenuptial agreement that is signed prior to the marriage. A prenuptial agreement is a valid contract and is generally honored by courts, which allows spouses to decide their financial rights and responsibilities instead of state law and can protect against debts of the other spouse. The prenuptial agreement is entered into prior to the marriage. However, most states allow you to waive the prenuptial agreement by later showing your intent. Some states do not follow this rule.

Another way to decrease the amount of your spouse's spousal share is by a written agreement entered into by both spouses after the marriage to waive their share of the other spouse's estate. This is, generally, honored by courts, unless the surviving spouse can show that the document was signed under duress or coercion.

In some states, the spousal share can be decreased by owning the property in joint tenancy with someone other than the spouse or by placing the property into a trust. In some states, you can name someone other than your spouse in a life insurance policy.

D. Rules Governing Your Primary Home

The law commonly refers to your primary home as your *homestead*, and generally provides the homestead great protection. If you have a spouse and/or minor children, the laws in your state may not allow you to leave your homestead to anyone other than your spouse and/or minor children. If you are divorced, with minor children, then your homestead will be left to your children. In some states, the homestead is protected to the point that creditors can't attach to the house. It is also worth noting that creditors will not be able to attach to *exempt property*, which includes furniture, furnishings, appliances, and cars titled in your name that are regularly used by you, your spouse, and/or minor children. Exempt property first goes to the surviving spouse and then to the minor children.

E.   Bank Accounts

The money in your bank account is considered property and will be subject to probate like any other property you own. There are ways of setting up bank accounts that will avoid probate.

Joint tenancy with right of survivorship: One way to guarantee that one person will inherit all of the funds in your bank account is to set up a joint tenancy with right of survivorship bank account. Just like joint tenancy with rights of survivorship of survivors in real property, the surviving owner will automatically get ownership of the entire account upon your death. Also, if you do create a joint tenancy, the other parties can take out as much money as they want without regard to how much they have contributed.

Payable on death bank accounts: If you have a specific person you would like to leave money to, creating a *payable on death bank account* is a great way of accomplishing that. This is a bank account that is kept separate from the rest of your estate, but within your exclusive control, until your death. The money you deposit in the bank account will be held in trust for the named beneficiary you choose. The account can be a checking, savings, money market, or certificate of deposit (CD) account. A payable on death account is created by filling out a form at the bank. Note that banks may use the term payable on death (POD), transfer on death (TOD), bank trust, or, the most commonly used term, *Totten trust*. You can think of this type of account as the most cost effective way of creating a trust.

Payable on death securities: Stocks, bonds, mutual funds, and other similar financial instruments can all be payable on death securities. The vast majority of states have passed a law called the Uniform TOD Securities Registration Act. To be valid, the security must be correctly registered. The brokerage firm that handles your account does the registration. If your state has not passed the law, you can move your securities into a state that has passed the law.

F.   Life Insurance

If you name a beneficiary on your life insurance policy, it will not go through probate, but it will still be subject to estate taxes. The life insurance policy will pay directly to your named beneficiary. A life insurance policy is a contract between you and the insurance company where you promise to pay premiums and the insurance company promises to pay your named beneficiaries upon your death. Upon your death, your beneficiary will be required to fill out some paperwork and provide the insurance company a copy of your death certificate.

If you have named minor children as beneficiaries, generally, the life insurance policy will pay directly into a child's trust account. However, some insurance policies will not allow you to name minor children as beneficiaries, so it's important to check your insurance policy. If your insurance policy does not allow you to name minor children as beneficiaries then you can either:

- create a living trust, the beneficiaries of which are the minor children, and then name the living trust as the beneficiary of your life insurance policy, to be paid out immediately upon your death, or
- name a guardian to manage the property that will be inherited by the minor children.

Any life insurance proceeds will be subject to an estate tax. To avoid this, the life insurance policy will need to be owned by someone other than yourself (the decedent). For example, your daughter can purchase the policy on your behalf. Note that there may be certain gift tax consequences.

G. Property of Minor Children

If you have no surviving spouse, then your minor children will get the homestead as well as all of the furnishings in the house. Your minor children are also entitled to get a *family allowance*, which is controlled by state law. Money in a joint payable on death bank account is not part of a family allowance.

The problem is that, under the eyes of the law, minors are not allowed to own property without adult supervision. If you have minor children, you have to make the necessary arrangements to take care of your minor children, through a will or trusts, or the court will appoint someone, called a court-appointed guardian to do so. If the court makes the decisions, then a portion of your estate will be used to pay for the court appointed services.

When creating your will and/or trusts for your minor children, you must take into consideration the amount of money that you are leaving to them, and also money that the minor children will receive from life insurance policies, gifts, and/or retirement plans that name the children as beneficiaries.

H. Debt on the Property in the Will

When there is still debt owed on property that is distributed by your will then the loan will, generally, need to be paid off before the property can pass to the beneficiary. However, property secured with a lien on the property, for example a house mortgage or car loan, is not required to be paid off to be transferred to a beneficiary. Most companies who hold the mortgage or loan on a piece of property will allow the passing of debt to the new owner without requiring the new owner to refinance.

The debt on your property will be paid from other property in your estate in the following order: first, probate fees, taxes, and funeral costs, next any remaining debt. If you want to transfer property in your will free and clear of any debts, then you can have your estate pay the debt off by including a *debt-forgiveness clause*. Generally, if you do not specify which property is to be given free of debt, then the executor will have the power to make that decision. You can exercise control over this by naming the specific property you want to be given free of debt with the debt-forgiveness clause. If you give property with a secured lien debt attached to it to the beneficiary, that beneficiary does not have to accept the property and can disclaim the property by contacting the executor in writing.

If you set up your estate in such a way that your property does not have to go through probate, then creditors cannot touch your property and any debts remaining on the estate will be wiped out if there is no property to sell to settle the accounts.

Federal student debt is generally discharged on your death, which means that the property in your estate will not be used to pay off your student debt when you die. However, your executor will need to notify the lender by providing a death certificate. Private student debt is not so easily discharged and will need to be paid by the estate before property can be distributed.

The executor is not personally liable for the debts and taxes of your estate, but they are responsible for filing the paperwork on your behalf. Generally, this requires the executor to use estate funds to pay one year taxes of the deceased, unless the property is complicated or there is likely to be a dispute at probate by a family member.

I.   Gifts

Before you die, you can gift your property to your beneficiaries. Any gift you make during your lifetime will not be subject to probate.

At the time of publication, Federal law allows an *annual exclusion* of gift tax, which is the amount you can give to someone in a calendar year (January 1 to December 31). You can gift

up to $14,000 as a single giver free of Federal taxes and married couples can combine their gifts to give a joint gift of $28,000 in a calendar year. For example, you want to give $14,000 to A, that gift would be tax free so long as you have not reached your lifetime gift amount which is $5.35 million. Any amount over this amount or over the lifetime exclusion will be taxed around 40%. If you want to give A $14,000 on December 31, 2013 and the same amount to A on January 1, 2014, then this would still be free of Federal taxes so long as you were still within your lifetime limit of $5.35 million and did not make any other gifts. If you are married, you can give jointly up to $28,000 in a calendar year. The receiver of the gift does not pay gift taxes, but the person who makes the gift is the one who is taxed.

To qualify as a gift, there can be no strings or stipulations to the person who receives the money. It is their money and they can do what they want with it.

J.   Retirement Accounts and Pensions

If, at the time of your death, there is any money left in your retirement account, your beneficiary will receive that money. The beneficiary should be registered with your brokerage house which creates a contract between you and the brokerage house which does not go through probate. If the brokerage house does not pay the beneficiary, then there is a breach of contract and your beneficiary can sue for nonpayment under contract law.

Retirement funds are subject to taxation. If you are considering naming someone other than your surviving spouse as a beneficiary, consult a lawyer or an accountant because the tax in this area can be complex.

Pension plans are not as common as they once were, although they do still exist. They are now called *defined benefit plans* because the benefit is set based on the employee's years of service and salary or seniority level. These traditional plans end at the death of the employee, unless it provides for the surviving spouse. In either event, the company needs to be notified of any deaths. If a death occurs mid-month, the company may require a refund of the remaining month's share payment.

Pension plans have been replaced with *defined contribution plans*, and include IRAs and employer-sponsored 401(k) plans. These accounts are funded directly from paychecks with pre-tax money and/or with separate contributions. After the age of 59.5 you can start taking out money without penalty. At age 70.5, you are required to take out money. When you die, and there is money in these accounts, they will go to the beneficiaries named in the plan administrator or with the financial institution. Beneficiaries of defined contribution plans are not named by will or trust.

K. Next Steps to Creating Your Will

The next step to creating your will, after identifying the people and property in your will, is to identify other things that you should include in your will.

5. Identifying Other Things to Include with Your Will

Now that you have identified the people and property that you want to include in your will, next, you should identify some of the other things that you want to include with your will. This will not only help your executor in the distribution of your estate, but it will help you identify important things you want to pass on in your will or otherwise. This chapter covers things that do not fit within the people or property categories from the previous two chapters.

A. Estate Records Organizer

As you begin the process of gathering all of the things that your loved ones may need after your death, creating an estate records organizer can help get you organized. The estate records organizer can be a notebook or simply some pages put together with information ranging from your address, Social Security Number, e-mail usernames, to various passwords, frequent flyer numbers, and the location of important documents. This information will help an executor, or anyone else, bring closure to your final arrangements. An estate records organizer is not required to be a part of your estate. You can leave the estate records organizer as part of your will or you can ask that the organizer only be given to the executor of the estate and then destroyed.

B. Medical/End of Life Decisions

Your will is a legal document that will be read, and adhered to, upon your death. During a medical emergency, your will won't be consulted. Instead, physicians and hospitals will want to reference a separate document, called a living will, to determine what your emergency or end of life medical wishes are. State law allows you to create a document which will serve as instructions to medical professionals about how you wish to be treated should you become unable to give these directions yourself, for example, if you become incapacitated. State law also allows you to name/appoint someone to make medical decisions for you if/when a situation occurs that you did not address in your living will through a document called a healthcare power of attorney.

a) Living Will

A *living will*, sometimes referred to as a declaration to physicians, is a legal document that instructs healthcare professionals on how they should treat you in the event that you are incapacitated. In other words, a living will controls whether or not you want to be on prolonged life support. Every state recognizes the living will.

In a living will, you state how you want your healthcare needs to be met. For example, you can dictate whether you want to be put on artificial life support or dictate that you prefer not to be resuscitated, sometimes referred to as a DNR (Do Not Resuscitate).

The living will only takes effect if you are not able to make your own decisions. Alzheimer's or forgetfulness will not be enough to justify the use of a living will. Being unable to make your own decisions means you are unconscious in some form. So long as you can make your own decisions, the living will does not have any legal effect. That means that so long as you are able to make your own decisions, you are free to change your mind without having to change your living will.

Generally, two witnesses (three witnesses in Vermont) and a notary public are required to create a legally binding living will. The witnesses must be:

- at least 19 years of age, but a few states allow someone who is 18,
- of "sound mind" and able to understand the nature of the document they are signing,
- unaffiliated with your attending physician, the medical facility, or a patient of the attending physician or medical facility,
- someone not financially responsible for your healthcare costs,
- someone other than a beneficiary in your will or who has any claim to a portion of your estate upon your death, and
- unpaid.

In a few states, if you are in a hospital, nursing home, boarding facility, or other healthcare facility when you create the living will, a patient advocate, director of the facility, or patient ombudsman is required to be a third witness.

If your wishes change, it is important to change your living will because if you are not able to make your own decisions, it will be difficult for anyone to contradict the living will.

Every state allows you to revoke your living will. Witnesses are not required to revoke. States vary in what they require for revocation, but generally allow revocation by:

- destroying the living will by tearing it up, burning it, or some other physical act, but simply scratching through the signature will not be enough,
- creating a separate document that revokes the living will or instructions to a third party to destroy the living will at your direction,
- some states allow for an oral revocation, but only in the presence of witnesses who will sign and date a written revocation of the living will, or
- gestures by non-verbal or written statements are allowed in some states regardless of the person's physical or mental conditions.

b) Healthcare Power of Attorney

A *healthcare power of attorney* gives another person the power to make your healthcare decisions. It must be in writing. The difference between the living will and the healthcare power of attorney is that in the living will you, yourself, state in advance how you want your healthcare situations to be handled if you become unable to do so, whereas the healthcare power of attorney gives that power to someone else. It is impossible to plan for every possible scenario. The healthcare power of attorney fills in the gaps.

The healthcare power of attorney and the living will work together. What you want to do is create a living will to make the major decisions on the most common healthcare issues and then designate someone else to make the remaining decisions regarding your healthcare. The healthcare power of attorney takes effect when you become unable to make your own decisions. Therefore, you should choose someone trustworthy who knows and understands your wishes. It is important to be as clear as possible about your medical preferences because the court is reluctant to go against the decisions made by your power of attorney; these decisions include withholding medical care, medication, food, and even water.

The person who you select to have your healthcare power of attorney will have the power to sign documents on your behalf, saying that they have your permission to sign their name in place of yours. The power remains in effect even if you become mentally insane, disabled, or incompetent.

In general, the same rules and laws regarding witnesses and revocation that apply to living wills also apply to the healthcare power of attorney. You should also name an alternate.

c) Organ, Tissue, and Body Donation

After you die, your loved ones and/or executor will be asked whether you wanted to donate your organs, or other body parts, for medical or scientific purposes. There are many reasons why a person would want, or not want, to donate their organs, tissue, and/or body such as for religious reasons. Whatever your personal reasons are, you should make your wishes clear to your loved ones and executor.

Your organs can be used to save someone else's life. Your organs may be used for teaching medical students or for medical research and/or experimentation.

You can donate organs and tissue including your heart, liver, kidneys, pancreas, eyes (corneas), lungs, skin, and various tendons for transplant.

If you plan on donating your body to science, it may go to a university. Generally, once the university is done with your body, it will be cremated and your ashes will be scattered in a designated plot of land. You can also make other arrangements. Remember that just because you want your body to go to science does not mean that it will be accepted and therefore you should make alternative arrangements.

You can choose to donate just organs, just tissue, or your entire body. You can be as specific as you want to be about which specific organs and/or tissue you would, or would not, like to donate.

C. Financial Durable Power of Attorney

Much like the healthcare power of attorney, the *financial durable power of attorney* allows you to appoint someone to handle your financial matters in the event that you are unable to make your own decisions. The financial durable power of attorney will not take effect unless, or until, you are physically unable to make your own decisions. A financial durable power of attorney does not grant the power to make healthcare decisions; you will need to create a healthcare power of attorney if you would like someone to be able to make medical decisions.

The person you name as your financial durable power of attorney must be an adult. Generally, if you are married, you would want to name your spouse, unless your spouse is mentally or physically unable to do the task or there is the potential for conflict.

It is important to name someone that you not only trust, but who is good with money. You can limit the person's power in the way you feel is best. For example, you may not want the person to sell your car or house, or to not go into debt over a certain amount.

You can grant the power to:

- pay your bills, expenses, and taxes,
- collect and file for Social Security, Medicare, or other government programs,
- operate your small business,
- hire someone to represent you in court,
- make gifts or transfer your property into an already existing trust, or
- make banking transactions and retirement decisions.

The financial durable power of attorney ends when you die, the person with the power dies, the court invalidates the power (extremely rare), or when you revoke the power, which you can do so long as you are of "sound mind."

As always, you should name an alternate.

D. Social Security

When you die if you have worked long enough as specified by the Social Security Administration (SSA), your family may get some benefits. To get Social Security benefit, you, as well as the family member to receive the benefits, must qualify. Social Security benefits are determined by the SSA. You should have the paperwork. Your family or executor will need to file the appropriate papers.

Some of the benefits that your family may receive are a $225 one time lump sum payment and monthly paid benefits.

A $225 one time lump sum is paid, in order of priority, to the surviving spouse, and if there is no surviving spouse, then the lump sum will be paid to a child who is eligible for benefits on your record in the month of your death.

The surviving spouse is eligible if:

- you both were living together at the time of your death, or
- if you were living apart, the surviving spouse can still collect if the surviving spouse was receiving certain Social Security benefits (because of its complexity, this topic is beyond the scope

of this book; seek additional resources by contacting the SSA or an attorney).

Monthly paid benefits to your widow or widower, unmarried children, or a few others who may qualify. Payments may be made to:

- a widow or widower who is:
  - age 60 or older (age 50 or older if disabled),
  - at any age, but is caring for any of your (the deceased) surviving children under age 16, or
  - at any age, but is caring for any of your (the deceased) surviving children who are disabled.
- an unmarried child of yours (the deceased) who is:
  - under 18 years of age (or up to age 19 if the unmarried child is a full-time student in an elementary or secondary school), or
  - over 18 years of age and has disability that began before they were 22 years of age
- your (the deceased) stepchild, grandchild, step-grandchild, or adopted child under certain circumstances (because of its complexity this topic is beyond the scope of this book; seek additional resources by contacting the SSA or an attorney),
- your (the deceased) parents, age 62 or older, who were dependent on you for at least half of their support, or
- your (the deceased) surviving, divorced spouse if they:
  - are 62 years of age or older,
  - were married to you for at least 10 years,
  - have been divorced for two or more years,
  - unmarried, and

- are not by themselves, or with someone else, eligible for equal or greater Social Security benefits.

To find out if you qualify for Social Security benefits you should contact the SSA toll-free at 1-800-772-1213 (for the deaf or hard of hearing, call TTY number, 1-800-325-0778) between 7a.m. to 7p.m. Monday-Friday. Calling the SSA allows you to plan, as well as, ensure that your family gets the benefits you have worked for during your lifetime.

When you die, the SSA must be notified as soon as possible to start the process. Generally, the funeral director does this for you, and will need your Social Security number. If the funeral director does not do this, then the executor or any family member can make the report.

Once the SSA process has started, the SSA will need:

- a certified copy of your death certificate,
- a copy of your marriage certificate,
- the Social Security numbers of:
  - you,
  - the surviving spouse, and the divorced spouse in certain circumstances,
  - any of your surviving unmarried children under the age of 18 (19 if the unmarried child is a full-time student in an elementary or secondary school), or any unmarried child of yours who has a disability that began before they were 22 years of age,
  - stepchild, grandchild, step-grandchild, or adopted child under certain circumstances, and/or

- your parents who are older than 62 and who were dependent on you for at least half of their support.
- tax returns and W-2s for the past two years and information about your employer for the past two years.

E.   Death Certificates

A death certificate is legal proof that someone has died. A death certificate is required for various things including life, car, and homeowner's insurance policies, bank accounts, stocks, bonds, and mutual funds. The government uses them to stop Social Security payments and other benefits.

Death certificates are, generally, closed from general public records for a period of time, usually 25 to 50 years. You cannot just go to the local health department and get a copy of a person's death certificate without some reason or relationship to the deceased. This is to protect private information. Therefore, getting a death certificate requires specific information.

States differ as to what information is required to obtain a death certificate. However, states request most of the same information. The death certificate is usually handled by the funeral director in the place where you are buried or cremated.

The information requested includes basic information such as name, address, and Social Security number, but can include race, diseases, and level of education.

The executor of your estate should get about 20 copies of the death certificate, but may need more depending on your estate.

F.   Self-Proving Affidavits

A *self-proving affidavit* is as a document that affirms that your will was signed by you in the presences of the witnesses and the notary public who all, together, watched you sign the will and that you knew you were signing for the purpose of creating your will. The purpose of the self-proving affidavits is to allow the will to be admitted into probate court without needing to contact the witnesses to prove the authenticity of the will.

The notary public puts their mark on a separate paper that is attached to the will. Note: the notary public is not making any statements about the will itself and is not notarizing the will. The separate sheet of paper is needed as the notary public is notarizing only the self-proving affidavits that states that the will was signed and witnessed by two people. This distinction is important. A notary may be reluctant to notarize a will, which is not the same as notarizing the self-proving affidavits.

A Notary Public may have their own form that they use for a self-proving affidavit. You can use either form, but often a notary public will not have their own form for self-proving affidavits. In that case, there is one in the back of this book.

A will can be entered into probate without a self-proving affidavit. Without self-proving affidavits, the court will likely first make a determination about the authenticity of the will. This may mean calling the witnesses to testify. The self-proving affidavit makes the process easier.

State laws are not uniform in regard to what is required in self-proving affidavits. California treats the witness signatures as the self-proving affidavit and no separate affidavit is needed. New Hampshire does allow the use of self-proving affidavits but requires special language that is beyond the scope of this book. If you want a self-proving affidavit in New Hampshire you will need to consult a licensed lawyer in your area. Louisiana, Washington, D.C., Maryland, Ohio and Vermont do not recognize them. The rest do. In this book, there are three self-proving affidavits. Use the form for the corresponding states.

Self-Proving Affidavit 1: Alabama, Alaska, Arizona, Arkansas, Colorado, Connecticut, Hawaii, Idaho, Illinois, Indiana, Maine, Michigan, Minnesota, Mississippi, Montana, Nebraska, Nevada, New Mexico, New York, North Dakota, Oregon, South Carolina, South Dakota, Tennessee, Utah, Virginia, Washington (State), West Virginia, or Wisconsin.

Self-Proving Affidavit 2: Delaware, Florida, Georgia, Iowa, Kansas, Kentucky, Massachusetts, Missouri, New Jersey, North Carolina, Oklahoma, Pennsylvania, Rhode Island, or Wyoming.

Self-Proving Affidavit 3: Texas.

G.   Ethical Will

An *ethical will* has no legal effect because it is not a will, but is rather a statement you make in writing that your executor passes on to loved ones. It is sometimes called a *legacy letter*.

The ethical will can be in the form of a:

- letter, a sentence, or any other statement you wish to make,
- diary or journal that you have kept over time,
- video so your loved ones can see and hear your voice, or
- special care package you leave for each of your loved ones.

You can have the executor keep the contents of the documents private so only the beneficiary that the ethical will is addressed to knows what is inside. You can choose how and what you want to say. The idea is to say something you:

- thought you would have the rest of your life to say,
- were unable or afraid to say during your lifetime,
- to help your loved ones cope with your passing,
- explain the process of what will happen now that you have died, and
- want to pass on such as knowledge and advice you have gained over the years.

H.   Explanation Letters

An *explanation letter* can help resolve disputes. Because your will does not generally provide information about why you distributed your property in the way that you did, the explanation letter can help fill that gap.

The explanation letter can detail what you hope your beneficiaries will do with your property once you pass. While it has no legal effect, the explanation letter may be used in court where there is a dispute.

The explanation letter can be combined with your ethical will to provide some closure and understanding of your last wishes.

I. Inform the World of Your Death

One of the jobs of the executor will be to inform the world that you have died. Your executor should have ready access to the people you want to be contacted, along with any message you want to leave them.

Also, you will want to create a biographical information sheet about yourself. This sheet should include things like where you were born, what you enjoyed about life, and any special people, places, and memories you have. You may want to include information about who your parents, grandparents, and other relatives were to pass on that knowledge to the next generation.

When your executor informs the world of your death, the biographical information you put together should help your executor inform the world about your life. This section focuses on how your executor will go about informing the world of your death, based on the information you leave behind.

a) Funeral, Cremation, and Memorial Services

Most people pay for their funeral, cremation, and memorial services on their own, by either purchasing an insurance policy, or paying for the arrangements ahead of time. If you do this, then you need to leave a copy of your contract and other information for the executor about these arrangements.

The difference between a funeral service and a memorial service is that at a funeral service the body is present whereas with a memorial service the body is not because it has been cremated or is otherwise unavailable. After the funeral service, the body is buried. Cremation is the burning of the body and the scattering of the ashes in accordance with your wishes, either over a grave or in some body of water like a river.

Issues you may wish to address:

- who should attend, including family, friends, and religious clergy,
- where and what time of day you want the ceremony,
- gravestone inscription,
- flowers to mark your grave,
- your preference for burial or cremation, and if you have a funeral ceremony whether it should be open or closed casket,
- any pallbearers,
- transportation to the grave and if you want a graveside ceremony,
- reception afterwards to celebrate your life, or
- any special requests such as a last song or prayer.

b) Newspaper Obituary Information

Newspapers and a few other publications print obituaries. You may wish to have your obituary published in your local newspaper or a larger publication. You may want to write your own obituary. If you don't want to draft the full version, you can draft an outline of things you want said or not said.

An obituary normally includes:

- a picture,
- your full name,
- place and date of birth and death,
- place, date, and time of any service held in your honor, as well as whoever is invited,
- who survives you,
- where you will be buried or where your ashes will be scattered,
- details about your life accomplishments,
- awards,
- education,
- military service,
- membership and activity in the community or religious organizations,
- where people can send flowers and gifts,
- hobbies, or
- any other message or statement you wish to make.

J. Next Steps to Creating Your Will

Before you start to create your will, you need to get organized. If you have all of the information you need in front of you, you will spend less time creating your will. Complete the Estate Records Organizer. Then begin creating your will using the sample will in this book.

III. Trusts

1. Introduction to Creating Your Own Trust

One of the fastest ways to transfer property after your death is through a trust because a trust is not required to go through probate. In addition to avoiding probate costs, a trust lets you control who will receive property after you die. This section provides information you need to create your own trust.

The trusts in this book are for living trusts and can be used by single and married couples, small or moderate estates that are worth less than $2 million.

To create a trust you do not always need a lawyer, especially for simple living trusts. All you really need is a little bit of intelligence and the right information.

If you do decide to retain a lawyer after looking through this book, then this book can still provide valuable information to help keep you informed as to what your lawyer is doing regarding your property.

Before you actually start filling out the living trust forms included in this book, it is important to understand some basic information about the functions and uses of trusts. Then you can start to identify the property you want to put into your trust and the people who you want to name as beneficiaries and trustees.

Planning your trust before you begin can help you to think about what are some of the things a trust can and cannot do for your estate. To make a trust you will need to educate yourself on the options you have when creating your trust.

The following chart shows the steps to create your own living trust using this book. This trusts section is organized in this layout.

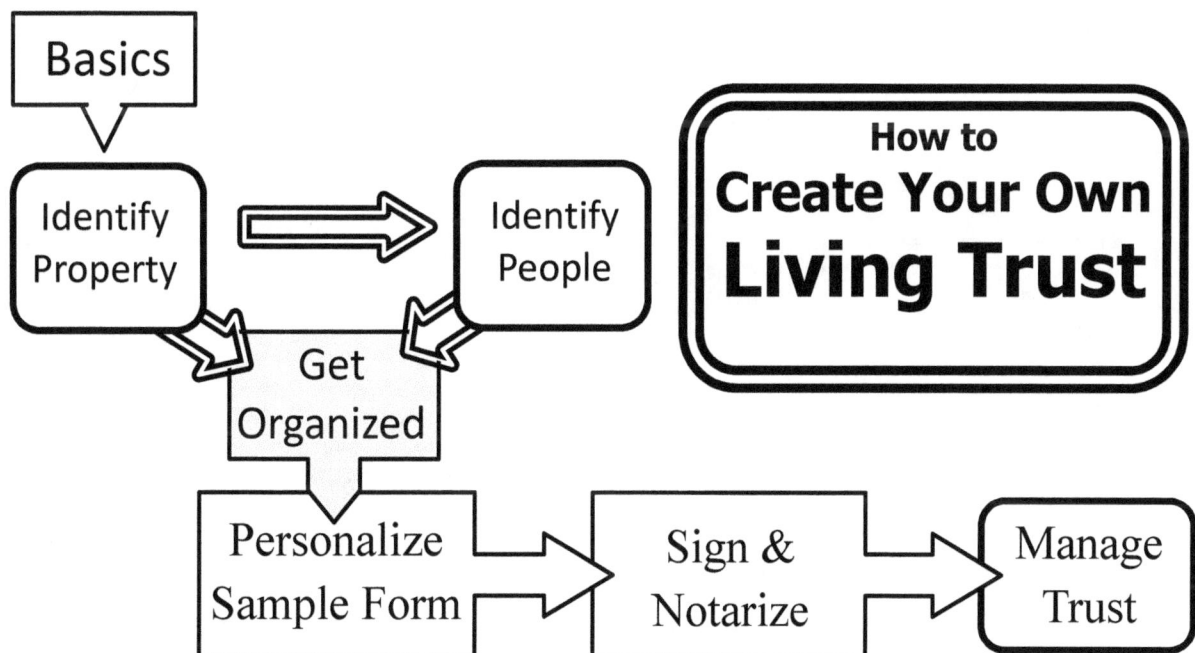

Basics

Identify Property → Identify People

Get Organized

Personalize Sample Form → Sign & Notarize → Manage Trust

How to Create Your Own Living Trust

2. Basics—Functions and Uses of Trusts

The first step to creating your trust is to understand what a trust is and why you are creating it. This chapter takes you through the basics of trusts. Along with explaining the basic functions of a trust, this chapter will help you determine what type of trust you need, and what, if any, additional resources you might need.

A. What's a Trust?

A trust is an abstract idea and requires some "legal fiction" meaning there is nothing that can be touched or seen, but does exist as far as the law is concerned. A *trust* is defined as the placing of confidence in a person, called a *trustee*, for the purpose of making the trustee the owner of property, to hold or use the property for the benefit of one or more other people, as directed by the creator of the trust. Once your trust is created, the trustee, not you, are the legal owners of the property in the trust. You can name multiple trustees to the same or different trusts.

B. Who Can Create a Trust?

The person who is the creator of the trust is referred to as the *settlor, grantor,* or *trustor.* The settlor exercises no control over the property after the trust is created and a list of rules governing how the property in the trust is to be managed and distributed will guide the trustee to carry out the settlor's wishes.

A settlor must be at least 18 years of age and have the rights to ownership in the property. The property can be shared with another person. If the property that is put into trust is shared, then only the settlor's share of the property can be put into the trust and no more because the settlor cannot give more than the settlor owns.

C. What Does a Trust Require?

A trust requires that you put property into it and that you name beneficiaries to receive the property. The type of property that you can put into the trust, your marital status, and when the trust will be created will determine what type of trust you need. Putting property in trust means the completion of documents that name the property to be transferred into the trust. The document must make a declaration to place the property in the trust of the trustee for the purposes laid out in the document. The date the property is transferred can be either the date of completing the documents that create the trust or at a later date, such as on your death.

The documents to create a trust must be:

- signed by the creator(s) who is/are of "sound mind" at the time of signing, and
- notarized.

Witnesses are only required in Florida.

D. What a Trust Can Do for You

Avoid probate. The property that is placed into the trust avoids probate because when the trust is created, the trustee is the lawful owner off the property in the trust, not you.

Reduce estate taxes. If used correctly, a trust can be used to reduce estate taxes. However, this really only applies to really large estates. As of 2013, that would mean estates greater than $5.35 million.

Provide for your minor child(ren). A trust can be used to provide for you minor child (ren) by providing them with trust property for medical, education, and living expenses. A trust for minor child(ren) will also manage the property in the trust for the child(ren) until they reach the age of majority (usually 18) or the age specified in the terms of the trust.

Quickly distribute property. Probate can take months and in some cases, years. A trust can quickly distribute trust property to the named beneficiaries after your death because it does not require court approval before distributing it.

Keep property distribution of property private. A trust can allow you to keep the property you keep in the trust and its distribution private because the trust does not need court approval, there is no disclosure requirement to anyone other than the government. However, many states require disclosure to family members of all trusts created and distributed by your estate.

Provide an alternative to creating a will. Creating a trust can also be used as an alternative to creating a will by naming all of your property in a trust. If you have no property left over, then there is no need for a will. We recommend you create both, a will and a trust.

E. What a Trust Cannot Do for You

Eliminate estate taxes. Estate taxes can be reduced or delayed, but a trust property that is disturbed is still subject to taxes. There is always a taxpayer.

Keep distributions completely private. Most states require the trust be disclosed to family members. Also, real estate transfers must be recorded in public records. Any lawsuits involving the trust will be made public.

Cut family completely out of your estate. A trust, like a will, can be contested by your heirs. Although a trust does not go through probate, an heir who wants to contest a trust you have left to another heir can do so under the same theory of law as they could under a will. Most states require disclosure to family members.

F. How to Change an Existing Trust

An existing trust may not always be changed depending on what type of trust has been created.

Living trust. A living trust can be changed because it is a trust you create while you are still alive and add property to it during your lifetime. You can remove property as you want by making changes to trust Schedule or codicil. The changes made by codicil should be minor changes.

Totten trust. A Totten trust can be changed because you are free to add or remove money from the bank account. By closing or removing all of the money you can change it. You can also change who you name as the beneficiary. There is no requirement to inform a beneficiary that they have been named as a beneficiary.

Minor child(ren)'s trust. A child(ren)'s trust once it has been created is very difficult to change by the person who created it because the trust then is owned by the trustees until the child(ren) reach the age specified by the trust.

G.   Types of Trusts

There are many types of trusts. Below are a few examples of trusts that you can create instead of, or along with, your will.

a)   Testamentary Trust

A *testamentary trust*, sometimes called a *will trust*, is a trust that you create in your will by stating that on your death, the trust is to be created. It cannot be created until after your death. The testamentary trust is created by your trustee or the person appointed by a probate court to handle your final arrangements.

These trusts protect against creditors, reduce taxes, and allow you to have some control over how your property will be disturbed upon your death.

b)   Living Trust

A *living trust* is a trust where the creator of the trust acts as the trustee of their own trust until their death, when the property is distributed according to the terms set out in the trust. The living trust is also called an *inter-vivos* or *revocable trust*. The creator of the trust can change and destroy the trust prior to their death, but, after their death, the trust is irrevocable. The trust does not go through probate and passes automatically to the named beneficiaries. You need to name an alternate trustee to manage the trust after you die. The main disadvantage of creating this type of trust, instead of a will, is that the trust requires a lot of management. The only property that will be subject to the trust is property that you specifically designate to the trust. Any property that you do not specifically put in the trust will pass according to your will or by state law.

i.   Individual Living Trust

If you are unmarried, you can use a living trust to leave all or part of your property to the named beneficiaries. You can also use it to create a trust for any minor child(ren) you may have.

If you are married, you can use the individual living trust if you most of your property is owned individually. This is especially true for newly married couples.

ii.   Married Living Trust

Married couples have special considerations because the property that they owned is generally owned together. Both spouses can agree to leave all other their property to the other who survives them and then after the surviving spouse's death to the named beneficiary. Both the husband and wife are the creators of the trust and are also the trustees. You can also use it to create a trust for any minor child(ren).

1.   Simple Married Living Trust

For most married couples, the simple married living makes the most sense. Each member of the couple acts as a co-grantor and co-trustee of the trust. However, each person may choose any beneficiary they may desire for their share of commonly owned property and for individually owned property in the trust. Both will have control over all of the property in the trust. Either person may revoke the trust at any time. If that happens, the ownership of the property returns to where it was before the trust was created.

When one of the spouses dies, the property originally contributed by that spouse will be distributed. Any property distributed to the surviving spouse will remain in the trust. The trust then continues until the death of the second spouse. The surviving spouse will then own all of the trust property and can distribute to the beneficiaries they wish regardless of which spouse brought the property into the trust originally.

2.   AB Living Trust

If you want to make sure that each spouse's property goes to their separate beneficiaries regardless of which spouse dies first, an AB living trust may be a better choice than a married living trust or a simple will. One of the primary reasons you would want to create an AB living trust is because it keeps the estate of the deceased spouse legally separate from the estate of the surviving spouse, while allowing the surviving spouse to benefit from the deceased spouse's property. This can be crucial for combined estates that are over the estate tax threshold.

With an *AB living trust*, or sometimes called an *exemption* or *bypass* trust, the property contributed to the trust by the first spouse to die will be distributed to the first spouse's beneficiaries after the death of the surviving spouse. The surviving spouse cannot change the beneficiaries of the deceased spouse's trust property. The surviving spouse will retain control and enjoyment of the property for their lifetime.

In this trust, both spouse list out their separate property and their beneficiaries. They also name the property that is shared. This meets the legal requirement that the property be separated. Upon the death of the first spouse, their separate property is put into trust A and the surviving spouse's property is put into trust B. The surviving spouse still retains full use of all property in both trusts. Upon the death of the surviving spouse, both trusts are distributed according to the named beneficiaries.

3.   AB Disclaimer Living Trust

The AB disclaimer living trust is very similar to the AB living trust except in the *AB disclaimer living trust*, rather than requiring that upon the first spouse's death, trust B be created and requiring that it be funded with all or a portion of the deceased spouse's estate under a marital deduction formula, the disclaimer trust leaves the decision as to whether to create such a trust until the death of the first spouse because the surviving spouse may not need the marital deduction tax advantage.

c)   Marital Trust

A *marital trust*, also called a *marital deduction trust* or an *"A" trust*, is created to take advantage of the Federal marital deduction which allows one spouse to transfer all of their property to the other spouse, in their lifetime, without being taxed. After death, transfers to the surviving spouse are subject to estate taxes. To qualify for the marital deduction, only the surviving spouse can be the beneficiary of the trust and must have the right to receive income from the trust during his or her lifetime. No matter how valuable the property in the trust is, even if it exceeds

that year's Federal estate tax exemption amount, your spouse won't owe any Federal estate taxes on that property. The surviving spouse does not necessarily have to take distributions of income unless required to do so by the terms of the trust. Since the trust property were not taxed at the first spouse's death, whatever remains in the trust at the death of the surviving spouse is subject to taxation in that spouse's estate. Only after your death, will your spouse has the right to use the property in the trust. The surviving spouse only gets a general power of appointment to allow the surviving spouse to control the ultimate distribution of the trust property and to modify the way property are distributed at his or her death, if your spouse so chooses.

d)   Totten Trust

A *Totten trust*, also called a *Payable on Death (POD) account*, is where one person adds money to a bank account that designates that whatever is in the account when they die, will be passed on to the named beneficiary. You can revoke the account at any time until your death or close the account. The bank account can be used as you normal do. To create a Totten trust you only need to complete a form with your bank. The form is retained by your bank and you will get a copy as well. The beneficiary does not need to be informed or give consent for you to name them as a beneficiary. At the death of the creator of the Totten trust, the funds automatically become the property of the named beneficiary.

e) Child(ren)'s Trust

A *child(ren)'s trust* is a trust created for child(ren), generally, by parents, to be managed by an adult until the child(ren) reach a certain age. The age can be any age you choose such as 25 or 40. The trusts in this book use the age of 35, but this can be changed to any age you choose. This trust is created for the benefit of minor child(ren) who, at the age of 18, would no longer be under the care of a guardian, but their parents/creators think it is in the child(ren)'s best interest to have the trust property managed beyond the child(ren)'s 18th birthday. You can name the same person as both the guardian of your child(ren) and as the trustee of your child(ren)'s trust. You do not have to name your surviving spouse. You should also name an alternate trustee.

You may also choose to name a property guardian for the property you leave to your minor child(ren). Property guardians are required to report to the court, about the property they manage, on a regular basis. Property guardian's authority to manage the property is governed/limited by state laws. The property guardian must turn over all property to the child when that child reaches the age of majority (usually 18).

The trustee is authorized to spend up to the amount in the trust for the well-being of the child(ren), including medical expenses, education, and maintenance. The trustee is responsible for investing trust property, paying taxes on behalf of the child(ren), and using the trust property to meet the child(ren)'s needs. The court is generally not involved in the trustee's decision making.

3. Identifying the Property and People in Your Trust

Once you understand the basic functions of a trust, your next step is to understand the property and people you can name as part of your trust. In this chapter, you will learn about the different property and people in your trust.

A. Property

Unlike the will where you would want to think about the people first, in a trust it makes more sense to start by thinking about what property that you want to put into your trust because the trust does not need to contain all of the property in your estate.

a) Real Estate

You can transfer real estate into a living trust to avoid probate. If you own the real estate as joint tenants or tenancy by the entirety you are already avoid probate so it may not make sense to create a living trust with your real estate in it. One of the other reasons to leave real estate in a living trust where there are joint owners (but not with a joint tenancy because of the rights of survivorship) is to provide for who will receive the real estate in the event that both owners die at the same time.

You can put real estate in an AB trust or AB disclaimer trust and potentially reduce tax liability because the real estate will be legally separate from the property of the surviving spouse.

If you do place real estate into a living trust, you do not need to notify your insurance company including your home owner's insurance, or the IRS because you are still the owner of the house during your lifetime.

b) Non-Real Estate

You can put into the trust almost any non-real estate property into your living trust that is legally owned by you. You must own some share of the property, but do not have to be in actual possession of the property.

Stocks and other securities. Stocks and other securities can be transferred into a living trust. Most brokerage accounts are familiar with living trusts to make the transfer. Once into the trust, all of the stocks and dividends are owned by the trust and you are the trustee so you will retain control. But, individual stock certificates will require you to get certificates issued in the trust's name. U.S. treasury bills can be placed into a living trust.

Money market accounts and bank accounts. You can put money market accounts and bank accounts into either a Totten trust or into a living will. A Totten trust does not usually allow you to name alternate beneficiaries. If you name more than one beneficiary in a Totten trust and one of your beneficiaries dies, then the remaining beneficiaries will split the amount in the trust with nothing going to the deceased or the deceased's estate.

Copyrights, patents, and royalties. You can transfer your right to any copyrights, patents, and future royalties you own into a living trust.

Minerals, oil, and gas interests. These are more complicated and you should seek the advice of a licensed attorney on adding these to your living trust.

c) Property That Should Not Be Put Into Your Living Trust

Cash. Cash cannot be put into a trust. Simply listing it will not work. You can put it in a bank account and either create a Totten trust or put the bank account into a living trust.

Retirement accounts. You should not put IRAs, 401(k)s, or profit sharing plans into a living trust, and in some cases, it is illegal to do so. Generally, you can name a beneficiary to avoid probate so there is no reason to put the accounts into a living trust.

Annuities. An annuity will generally allow you to name a beneficiary as part of the contract. The money is received by the beneficiary outside of probate.

Life insurance. When you bought the life insurance, you named the beneficiaries.

Vehicles. Some insurance companies will not insure you if the vehicle is in a trust. Most states allow a vehicle to be registered in joint tenancy to avoid probate. "Transfer-on-death" vehicle registration which avoids probate is available in California, Connecticut, Kansas, Missouri, and Ohio.

Checking account. You can put a checking account into a living trust, but if do, then the checks will name the trust as the payer.

Joint tenancy property. Property held in joint tenancy does not go through probate, so there is no need to name it in your living trust.

Community property with rights of survivorship. States that are community property states do not require shared property in the marriage to go through probate, and Alaska, Arizona, California, Nevada, Texas, and Wisconsin expressly authorize spouses to own community property in this manner.

B. People

After you have determined what property you want to include in your trust, then you need to identify who you will name as beneficiaries and who will be the trustee to manage the property in the trust. Keep in mind that many, but not all, of the laws that applied to wills are also applied to trusts.

a) Beneficiaries

A *beneficiary* is person(s) or organizations that receive the property in a trust. They do not have to be U.S. citizens or residents. When you create a trust, naming a beneficiary is required. A beneficiary's interest in a trust varies depending on the type of trust that has been created.

Property that is received by beneficiaries is not subject to Federal income tax on the amount they receive, but if the property they receives interest after they receive it, then that portion of earned interest is taxable.

Primary beneficiary. This is the person or organization who you select to be the one who gets the property when you die. You can name multiple primary beneficiaries to share property.

Alternate beneficiary. You are not required, but should name an alternate beneficiary. An alternate beneficiary gets the property should the primary beneficiary die before you or rejects the property. You can name multiple alternate beneficiaries to share the property. Naming an alternate beneficiary for the alternate beneficiary is not generally done because if both the primary beneficiary and the alternate beneficiary die, the property in the trust will go to the residuary beneficiary named in the trust.

Residuary beneficiary. A residuary beneficiary receives the property that is left in the trust that is not specifically named to a primary or alternate beneficiary.

Alternate residuary beneficiary. Just like the alternate beneficiary, the alternate residuary beneficiary is not required, but you should name one. If the residuary beneficiary dies before you or rejects the property, then the property will pass to the alternate. Naming an alternate to the alternate is not generally done.

Minor Child(ren). If you name a beneficiary who is a minor (under 18), you must name an adult to manage the property in the trust on the minor's behalf because minor cannot own property or enter into contracts. The adult who manages the property for the minor can do so until the age of 18 or until a later age which you specify in the trust.

Child(ren) born after a trust has been created. Generally, the law expects parents to provide for their child(ren) including those that are born after the creation of a legal document. Although the laws generally only name wills, courts will extend the reach to trusts if the child has not been provided for elsewhere or appropriately. The reason is that courts presume that a parent did not intentionally leave out a child simply because they were born after the date a document is entered into. To account for this in your living trust you can add a codicil.

Grandchild(ren). There is no requirement that property be left to grandchild(ren), except in certain circumstances where the parents of the grandchild(ren) have died. In which case, the grandchild(ren) take the place of the parents.

Pets. The law does not allow a pet to own property, but you can name property in a trust to someone you know will look after the pet for you. The pet will not own the property and there is likely no legal remedy if the person you name does not carry out your wishes, so choose someone you can trust.

b) Trustees

A *trustee* is a person, or organization such as a bank, who is given control or powers of administration over property in trust, with a legal obligation to administer the property solely for the purposes specified by the creator of the trust. An executor gives property to a trustee to hold for a third person. For example, an executor might give property to a trustee to care for the property of a minor child. A trustee has a role similar to the executor, but where the executor's job ends when probate ends, a trustee's job and responsibilities can continue for years, to be determined by the nature of the trust that has been created. A trust is a way to hold property, under the care of the trustee, for the benefit of another, the distribution of which will be under the discretion of the trustee, according to the rules/obligations described by the creator of the trust which, in this case, would be the testator.

Trustees have legal title of the property in a trust and are authorized to buy and sell property for the benefit of the trust without the court's, or the beneficiaries', permission. A trustee has almost absolute power over the property so it is important to put some consideration into who you name as your trustee.

The trustee must keep the beneficiaries informed about what is happening with the trust account. This notice requires enough information to determine the activities of the trust, including accounting of losses, gains, and payments made out of the trust.

The trustee is entitled to be compensated for their services. While the trustee can be paid a reasonable amount for their services, they may not make a profit at the expense of the trust. This means that the trustee cannot make a commission that would be paid by a third party. For example, if the trustee acts as a sales agent, the trustee may not earn any sales commission. If you decide to hire a trust company, such as a bank, the annual fee is usually around 1% of the trust property. Family or friends may decide not to charge you anything, or they may decide to charge you more.

Naming multiple trustees is recommended because it helps to spread around the risk of dishonest or unreliable trustees. You can name trustees as co-trustees or you can name different trustees to look after different property.

It is also recommended that you have the trustees post surety bonds, which protects the trust property. A *surety bond* is paid by the trustee in the amount that roughly equals the value of the property that is in the trust. This helps protect against fraud or reckless mismanagement by the trustee. If the trustee acts honestly, and for the benefit of the trust, then the surety bond is returned to the trustee at the completion of the trust.

IV. Estate Records Organizer

1. People
    A.   My Information
    B.   Beneficiaries
    C.   Guardians for Minor Child
    D.   Pets
    E.   Others Who Depend On Me
    F.   Witnesses and Notary Public
    G.   Executor
    H.   Trustees

2. Property
    A.   Real Estate
    B.   Bank Accounts
    C.   Insurance and Annuities
    D.   Death Benefits
    E.   Trusts
    F.   Non-Real Estate Debt
    G.   Retirement Accounts and Pensions

3. Other Things
    A.   Organ, Tissue, and Body Donation
    B.   Inform the World of Your Death
        a)   Cremation or Burial, and Funeral and Memorial Services
        b)   Newspaper Obituary Information

Estate Records Organizer (Cover Page)

Name: _____   Date: _____

I have organized the following records:

<table>
<tr><td valign="top">

1. People

- ❑ A. My Information
- ❑ B. Beneficiaries
- ❑ C. Guardians for Minor Child(ren)
- ❑ D. Pets
- ❑ E. Others Who Depend on Me
- ❑ F. Witnesses and Notary Public
- ❑ G. Executor
- ❑ H. Trustees

</td><td valign="top">

2. Property

- ❑ A. Real Estate
- ❑ B. Bank Accounts
- ❑ C. Insurance and Annuities
- ❑ D. Death Benefits
- ❑ E. Trusts
- ❑ F. Non-Real Estate Debt
- ❑ G. Retirement Accounts and Pensions

</td><td valign="top">

3. Other Things

- ❑ A. Organ, Tissue, and Body Donation
  - B. Inform the World of Your Death
    - ❑ a) Cremation or Burial, and Funeral and Memorial Services
    - ❑ b) Newspaper Obituary Information-

</td></tr>
</table>

I have completed the following documents:

<table>
<tr><td valign="top">

1. Wills

- ❑ Last Will and Testament
- ❑ Self-Proving Affidavit
- ❑ Living Will
- ❑ Amendment
- ❑ Revocation
- ❑ Ethical Will
- ❑ Explanation Letter

</td><td valign="top">

2. Power of Attorney

- ❑ Healthcare—Durable
- ❑ Financial—Durable
- ❑ Minor Child Care—Limited
- ❑ Revocation

</td><td valign="top">

3. Trusts

Living Trust: (select one)
- ❑ Simple One Person
- ❑ Simple Shared
- ❑ AB (With Disclaimer Statement: ❑No ❑Yes)
- ❑ Florida Witness Statement
- ❑ Assignment of Property to a Living Trust
- ❑ Affidavit of Assumption of Duties by Successor Trustee
- ❑ Amendment
- ❑ Revocation

</td></tr>
</table>

1. People

A. My Information

Full legal (and maiden) name: _____

Address: _____

SSN: _____ DOB: _____ Phone: _____

I have a: Location:

❑ Birth certificate   _____

❑ Adoption papers   _____

❑ Social Security card _____

❑ Driver's license   _____

❑ Passport   (Country_____) _____

❑ Divorce papers   _____

❑ Stocks   _____

❑ Bonds   _____

❑ Certificate of Deposits _____

❑ _____   _____

❑ _____   _____

❑ _____   _____

E-mail address: _____@_____ Password: _____

E-mail address: _____@_____ Password: _____

Social media: ❑ Facebook Username: _____ Password: _____

❑ _____ Username: _____ Password: _____

❑ _____ Username: _____ Password: _____

Armed Forces: ❑ No ❑ Yes, branch/unit: _____

_____V.A. claims number: _____

Discharge: ❑ Active ❑ Retired ❑ Other: _____

Education: _____

_____

_____

_____

Diseases/illness/allergies that your doctors/family should know about: _____

_____

Doctor's name: Dr._____ Phone: _____

Address: _____

Past two years tax returns and W-2s located: _____

Employers for past five years:

Organization name: _____ Phone: _____

Contact Person (name and title): _____

Address: _____

Dates of employment: _____ to _____ ❑ F/T ❑ P/T

Organization name: _____ Phone: _____

Contact Person (name and title): _____

Address: _____

Dates of employment: _____ to _____ ❑ F/T ❑ P/T

Organization name: _____ Phone: _____

Contact Person (name and title): _____

Address: _____

Dates of employment: _____ to _____ ❏ F/T ❏ P/T

Organization name: _____ Phone: _____

Contact Person (name and title): _____

Address: _____

Dates of employment: _____ to _____ ❏ F/T ❏ P/T

Mother's name (and maiden name): _____

Year of birth: _____ Place of birth: _____ Number of children: ____

Deceased: ❏ No ❏ Yes, cause: _____ Number of marriages: __

Family medical history: _____

_____

Ancestor information: _____

_____

Father's name: _____

Year of birth: _____ Place of birth: _____ Number of children: ____

Deceased: ❏ No ❏ Yes, cause: _____ Number of marriages: __

Family medical history: _____

_____

Ancestor information: _____

_____

B. Beneficiaries (including people and charitable organizations)

Type (select one): ❑ Primary ❑ Alternate Primary ❑ Residuary ❑ Alternate Residuary

Beneficiary name: _____ Phone: _____

Address: _____

Relation: _____ Description of property to be left: _____

_____

Location of property: _____

Property given by (select one): ❑ Will ❑ Trust ❑ Gift ❑ Other: _____

Shared: ❑ No ❑ Yes, percentage given: _____% shared with: _____

_____

Type (select one): ❑ Primary ❑ Alternate Primary ❑ Residuary ❑ Alternate Residuary

Beneficiary name: _____ Phone: _____

Address: _____

Relation: _____ Description of property to be left: _____

_____

Location of property: _____

Property given by (select one): ❑ Will ❑ Trust ❑ Gift ❑ Other: _____

Shared: ❑ No ❑ Yes, percentage given: _____% shared with: _____

_____

C. Guardians for Minor Child

Child's name: _____ Phone: _____

Address: _____

DOB: _____ SSN: _____ Relation: _____

Important documents located: _____

Any trust(s): ❏ No ❏ Yes, trust(s) name(s): _____

      Property held in trust: _____

Property not held in trust: _____

Doctor's name: Dr. _____ Phone: _____

      Address: _____

Special needs/allergies: _____

Personal guardian name: _____ Phone: _____

      Address: _____

Alternate personal guardian: _____ Phone: _____

      Address: _____

Property manager: ❏ No ❏ Yes, name: _____ Phone: _____

      Address: _____

D. Pets

Animal name: _____ Age: _____ Species: _____

Color(s)/marking(s)/distinction(s): _____

Spayed/neutered: ❑ No ❑ Yes   Diet/medication(s): _____

Shot(s)/license/important documents located: _____

Veterinarian name: Dr._____ Phone: _____

  Address: _____

New owner name: _____ Phone: _____

  Address: _____

Alternate name: _____ Phone: _____

  Address: _____

Other instructions: _____

Animal name: _____ Age: _____ Species: _____

Color(s)/marking(s)/distinction(s): _____

Spayed/neutered: ❑ No ❑ Yes   Diet/medication(s): _____

Shot(s)/license/important documents located: _____

Veterinarian name: Dr._____ Phone: _____

  Address: _____

New owner name: _____ Phone: _____

  Address: _____

Alternate name: _____ Phone: _____

  Address: _____

Other instructions: _____

E. Others Who Depend On Me

Name: _____ Phone: _____

Address: _____

Relation: _____ Location of documents: _____

Doctor's name: Dr. _____ Phone: _____

    Address: _____

Special needs/allergies: _____

Personal guardian name: _____ Phone: _____

    Address: _____

Alternate personal guardian: _____ Phone: _____

    Address: _____

Name: _____ Phone: _____

Address: _____

Relation: _____ Location of documents: _____

Doctor's name: Dr. _____ Phone: _____

    Address: _____

Special needs/allergies: _____

Personal guardian name: _____ Phone: _____

    Address: _____

Alternate personal guardian: _____ Phone: _____

    Address: _____

F.   Witnesses and Notary Public

Type (select one): ❑ Witness ❑ Notary Public (name of business: _____)

Name: _____ Phone: _____

Address: _____

Document(s) to which they are acting: _____

_____

Type (select one): ❑ Witness ❑ Notary Public (name of business: _____)

Name: _____ Phone: _____

Address: _____

Document(s) to which they are acting: _____

_____

Type (select one): ❑ Witness ❑ Notary Public (name of business: _____)

Name: _____ Phone: _____

Address: _____

Document(s) to which they are acting: _____

_____

Type (select one): ❑ Witness ❑ Notary Public (name of business: _____)

Name: _____ Phone: _____

Address: _____

Document(s) to which they are acting: _____

_____

G. Executor

Type (select one): ❑ Executor ❑ Alternate executor

Name: _____ Phone: _____

Address: _____

Shared responsibility: ❑ No ❑ Yes, with name: _____

    Address: _____

    Phone: _____

Type (select one): ❑ Executor ❑ Alternate executor

Name: _____ Phone: _____

Address: _____

Shared responsibility: ❑ No ❑ Yes, with name: _____

    Address: _____

    Phone: _____

Type (select one): ❑ Executor ❑ Alternate executor

Name: _____ Phone: _____

Address: _____

Shared responsibility: ❑ No ❑ Yes, with name: _____

    Address: _____

    Phone: _____

H. Trustees

Type (select one): ❑ Trustee ❑ Alternate Trustee

Name: _____ Phone: _____

Address: _____

Compensation: $_____ Duration: _____

Documents located: _____

Shared responsibility: ❑ No ❑ Yes, with name: _____

    Address: _____

    Phone: _____

Description of property in trust: _____

_____

_____

_____

_____

Instructions: _____

_____

_____

_____

2. Property

A. Real Estate

Type (select one): ❑ Homestead ❑ Other residence ❑ Commercial ❑ Other: _____

Address: _____

Name/description of property: _____

Location of documents/title: _____

Property given by (select one): ❑ Will ❑ Trust ❑ Gift ❑ Other: _____

Payoff all debts before distributing: ❑ No ❑ Yes, pay from: _____

Primary Beneficiary: _____ Phone: _____

    Address: _____

    Shared: ❑ No ❑ Yes, percentage given: _____% shared with_____

    _____

Alternate Primary Beneficiary: _____ Phone: _____

    Address: _____

    Shared: ❑ No ❑ Yes, percentage given: _____% shared with_____

    _____

Mortgage: ❑ No ❑ Yes, origination date: _____ Amount: $_____

    Estimated pay-off date: _____ Monthly payments: $_____

    Account number: _____ Auto pay enabled: ❑ No ❑ Yes

    Mortgagor holder/bank's name: _____

    Agent's name: _____ Phone: _____

    Address: _____

    Online username: _____ Password: _____

Equity line: ❑ No ❑ Yes, origination date: _____ Amount: $_____

Estimated pay-off date: _____ Monthly payments: $_____

Account number: _____ Auto pay enabled: ❑ No ❑ Yes

Equity holder/bank's name: _____

Agent's name: _____ Phone: _____

Address: _____

Online username: _____ Password: _____

Property manager: ❑ No ❑ Yes, name: _____ Phone: _____

Address: _____

Insurance policy: ❑ No ❑ Yes (see *Insurance and Annuities* section for more details)

Brief description/details: _____

B. Bank Accounts

Bank name: _____ Account number: _____

Contact name: _____ Phone: _____

Branch address: _____

Location of documents: _____

Online username: _____ Password: _____

Savings account: ❑ No ❑ Yes, account number: _____

    Joint account: ❑ No ❑ Yes, with: _____

Checking account: ❑ No ❑ Yes, account number: _____

    Joint account: ❑ No ❑ Yes, with: _____

    Checkbook: ❑ No ❑ Yes, location of checkbook: _____

Debit card: ❑ No ❑ Yes, number: _____ Expires: _____

    ❑ Visa ❑ MasterCard   ❑ Other card holders: _____

Direct deposit: ❑ No ❑ Yes, amount: $_____Frequency: ❑ Monthly ❑ Bi-Weekly
❑ Weekly ❑ Annual ❑ Other: _____

    Payment received from (name): _____

    Contact name: _____ Phone: _____

    Address: _____

Auto pay: ❑ No ❑ Yes, to/date(s) drafted: _____

_____

_____

Safety deposit box: ❑ No ❑ Yes, key location: _____ Code: _____

    Names on account: _____ Payment methods: _____

    Payment on Death set-up: ❑ No ❑ Yes, beneficiary: _

C. Insurance and Annuities

Type : ❑ Life ❑ Worker's compensation ❑ Health ❑ Medicare ❑ Medicaid ❑ Dental ❑ Vision
❑ Disability ❑ Long-term care ❑ Auto ❑ Home ❑ Renter's ❑ Military ❑ Annuity
❑ Other: _____

Coverage description: _____

_____

Location of documents: _____

Policy number: _____ Date issued: _____

Online username: _____ Password: _____

Status: ❑ Active ❑ Expired ❑ Discharged, reason: _____

Company/provider name: _____

    Agent name: _____ Phone: _____

    Branch address: _____

Part of employment: ❑ No ❑ Yes, employer name: _____

    Current employer: ❑ No (Reason for discharge: _____) ❑ Yes

    Contact name: _____ Phone: _____

    Address: _____

    Dates of employment: _____ to _____

D.   Death Benefits

Status (select one): ❑ Current ❑ Past ❑ Spouse ❑ Other: _____

Policy type (select one): ❑ Group life insurance ❑ Group health insurance (death benefits)
❑ COBRA ❑ Deferred compensation ❑ Credit union deposits ❑ Pension (survivors' benefits)
❑ Profit-sharing (survivors' benefits) ❑ Unpaid salary ❑ Other: _____

Coverage description: _____

_____

Location of documents: _____

Policy number: _____ Date issued: _____

Online username: _____ Password: _____

Status: ❑ Active ❑ Expired ❑ Discharged, reason: _____

Company/provider name: _____

   Agent name: _____ Phone: _____

   Branch address: _____

Part of employment: ❑ No ❑ Yes, employer name: _____

   Current employer: ❑ No (Reason for discharge: _____) ❑ Yes

   Contact name: _____ Phone: _____

   Address: _____

   Dates of employment: _____ to _____

If killed on the job, additional benefits may be paid to the family: ❑ No ❑ Yes, from: ❑ Worker's
   compensation ❑ Accidental travel insurance, common carrier insurance, tickets purchased
   by credit card ❑ Other: _____

E.   Trusts

Trust title: _____

Beneficiary: _____ Phone: _____

   Address: _____

Child's trust: ❏ No ❏ Yes, DOB: _____ SSN: _____

   Relation: _____

   Personal guardian(s) ❏ No ❏ Yes, name(s): _____

      Address: _____

      Phone: _____

Location of documents: _____

Description of trust property: _____

_____

_____

Trust instructions: _____

Preparer's name: _____ Phone: _____

   Address: _____

   Company: _____ Date prepared: _____

Trustee name: _____ Phone: _____

   Address: _____

Alternate Trustee name: _____ Phone: _____

   Address: _____

F.   Non-Real Estate Debt

Debt (select one): ❑ Credit Card ❑ Student ❑ Auto ❑ Other: _____

Status: ❑ Active ❑ Grace ❑ Deferred ❑ Other: _____

Company/provider name: _____

Contact name: _____ Phone: _____

Address: _____

Location of documents: _____

Account number: _____ Auto pay: ❑ No ❑ Yes, amount: $ _____

Monthly due date: _____ Monthly payments: $_____

Origination date: _____ Original amount: $_____

Estimated pay-off date: _____

Online username: _____ Password: _____

Debt (select one): ❑ Credit Card ❑ Student ❑ Auto ❑ Other: _____

Status: ❑ Active ❑ Grace ❑ Deferred ❑ Other: _____

Company/provider name: _____

Contact name: _____ Phone: _____

Address: _____

Location of documents: _____

Account number: _____ Auto pay: ❑ No ❑ Yes, amount: $ _____

Monthly due date: _____ Monthly payments: $_____

Origination date: _____ Original amount: $_____

Estimated pay-off date: _____

Online username: _____ Password: _____

G. Retirement Accounts and Pensions

Type (select one): ❑ 401(k) ❑ IRA ❑ Social Security ❑ Pension ❑ Other: _____

Status: (select one): ❑ Active ❑ Expired ❑ Receive payments

Location of documents: _____

Company name: _____ Contact Name: _____

Address: _____ Phone: _____

Account number: _____ Auto pay: ❑ No ❑ Yes, amount: $ _____

Type (select one): ❑ 401(k) ❑ IRA ❑ Social Security ❑ Pension ❑ Other: _____

Status: (select one): ❑ Active ❑ Expired ❑ Receive payments

Location of documents: _____

Company name: _____ Contact Name: _____

Address: _____ Phone: _____

Account number: _____ Auto pay: ❑ No ❑ Yes, amount: $ _____

Type (select one): ❑ 401(k) ❑ IRA ❑ Social Security ❑ Pension ❑ Other: _____

Status: (select one): ❑ Active ❑ Expired ❑ Receive payments

Location of documents: _____

Company name: _____ Contact Name: _____

Address: _____ Phone: _____

Account number: _____ Auto pay: ❑ No ❑ Yes, amount: $ _____

3. Other

A. Organ, Tissue, and Body Donation

I want to be a donor: ❑ No ❑ Yes, registered with: ❑ DMV ❑ Health department ❑ Other:

_____ ❑ Not registered, but I wish to be a donor

Donate my organs: ❑ No ❑ Yes (Only: ❑ Any organs ❑ Heart ❑ Liver ❑ Kidneys ❑ Pancreas

❑ Lungs ❑ Intestines ❑ Anything, but: _____

_____)

Donate my tissue: ❑ No ❑ Yes (Only: ❑ Any tissue ❑ Heart valves ❑ Eyes-corneas ❑ Tendons

❑ Bone ❑ Skin ❑ Veins ❑ Anything, but _____

_____)

Donate body for medical education/research: ❑ No ❑ Yes

Location of documents: _____

Arrangements made: ❑ No ❑ Yes, for _____

Organization name: _____ Phone: _____

Contact person: _____ Date arrangements made: _____

Address: _____

B. Inform the World of Your Death
a) Cremation or Burial, and Funeral and Memorial Services

Cremation or Burial (select one)

❑ Cremated (❑ Columbarium niche ❑ In the ground ❑ Scattered over: _____

_____

   ❑ Ashes to, name: _____ Phone: _____

      Address: _____

   ❑ Urn: ❑ No ❑ Yes, type: ❑ Ceramic ❑ Stone: _____

      ❑ Other: _____

      Budget: $_____ at least: $_____ ❑ No budget)

[OR]

❑ Buried (❑ Below ground ❑ Above ground) Plot location: _____

_____

   Burial marker: ❑ No ❑ Yes, budget: ❑ $_____ at least: $_____ ❑ Any

      Size: ❑ Any ❑ Same size as neighbors' ❑ Large

      Statue material: ❑ Any ❑ Stone: _____

         ❑ Other: _____

      Design: ❑ Any ❑ _____

_____

      Epitaph: ❑ No ❑ Yes, inscription: _____

_____

_____

   Casket: budget: Stay Under: $_____ At least: $_____ ❑ Any

Material: ❑ Any ❑ Wood: _____

❑ Other: _____

Exterior Finish and Design: ❑ Any ❑ Other: _____

_____

_____)

Arrangements made: ❑ No ❑ Yes, for: _____

Funeral home name: _____ Phone: _____

Contact person: _____ Date arrangements made: _____

Address: _____

Location of documents: _____

Time of cremation/burial (select one): ❑ After service ❑ Before service ❑ Immediately after I die
Embalm (select one): ❑ No ❑ Yes ❑ No preference
Attire to be cremated/buried in (select one): ❑ Traditional ❑ Any ❑ As follows: _____

_____

_____

Funeral and Memorial Services

Type of service: ❑ Religious ❑ Military ❑ Other: _____
❑ Open to the public ❑ Wake ❑ Open casket ❑ Body present ❑ Flowers ❑ Photograph
displayed ❑ Photograph location: _____ ❑ No preference

Budget: $_____   At least: $_____   ❑ Any
Time preference: ❑ Morning ❑ Afternoon   ❑ Evening ❑ Day preference: _____
Attire during service: ❑ Any ❑ Traditional ❑ Same as cremation/buried ❑ As follows: _____

_____

_____

Specific request(s): _____

_____

Arrangements made: ❏ No ❏ Yes, for: _____

Funeral home name: _____ Phone: _____

Contact person: _____ Date arrangements made: _____

Address: _____

Location of documents: _____

Eulogy

Eulogizer name: _____ Phone: _____

Address: _____

Eulogizer name: _____ Phone: _____

Address: _____

Eulogizer name: _____ Phone: _____

Address: _____

Readings

Name: _____ Phone: _____

Address: _____

Name: _____ Phone: _____

Address: _____

Name: _____ Phone: _____

Address: _____

Reception

Arrangements made: ❏ No ❏ Yes, for _____

Organization name: _____ Phone: _____

Contact person: _____ Date arrangements made: _____

Address: _____

Location of documents: _____

Immediately following funeral/memorial service: ❑ No ❑ Yes, then: _____

Budget: $_____   At least: $_____   ❑ Any

Time preference: ❑ Morning ❑ Afternoon ❑ Evening ❑ Day preference: _____

Specific request(s): _____

Type of reception: ❑ Religious ❑ Military ❑ Other: _____ ❑ Open to the public ❑ Wake ❑ Open casket ❑ Body present ❑ Flowers ❑ Photograph displayed ❑ Photograph location: _____ ❑ No preference

Food and Drinks: _____

_____

_____

_____

_____

_____

_____

Specific requests: _____

_____

_____

_____

Pallbearers and Alternate Pallbearers

❑ Pallbearer ❑ Alternate pallbearer ❑ Either

Name: _____ Phone: _____

Address: _____

❑ Pallbearer ❑ Alternate pallbearer ❑ Either

Name: _____ Phone: _____

Address: _____

❑ Pallbearer ❑ Alternate pallbearer ❑ Either

Name: _____ Phone: _____

Address: _____

❑ Pallbearer ❑ Alternate pallbearer ❑ Either

Name: _____ Phone: _____

Address: _____

❑ Pallbearer ❑ Alternate pallbearer ❑ Either

Name: _____ Phone: _____

Address: _____

❑ Pallbearer ❑ Alternate pallbearer ❑ Either

Name: _____ Phone: _____

Address: _____

❑ Pallbearer ❑ Alternate pallbearer ❑ Either

Name: _____ Phone: _____

Address: _____

b) Newspaper Obituary Information

I want my obituary published: ❏ No ❏ Yes, in the following publication(s): _____

_____

I have drafted a version: ❏ No ❏ Yes (see below)
The final version should be written by:

Name: _____ Phone: _____

Address: _____

I want a photograph included: ❏ No ❏ Yes, ❏ enclosed is the photo

Obituary Information

Name:	
Place of Birth:	
City:	
DOB:	
Spouse, children, grand-children, etc.:	
Military service:	
Organization and/or houses of worship mem-bership:	
Employment:	
Achievements:	
Education:	
Hobbies:	
Services Place Name and Address:	
Services date/time:	
Service conducted by:	
Flowers:	❏ Yes. Send To: ❏ No flowers ❏ But remembrance donations to:
Donations:	
Additional notes:	

V. Sample Will, Power Of Attorney, and Trust Forms

1. Wills

Last Will and Testament Checklist

❑ Make additional copies of any specific pages you may need or tear them out of the book.

❑ Read over the blank form.

❑ If there are parts of the form you do not understand, read the applicable section within this book.

❑ Make adjustments to the form to meet your needs. If the paragraph or portion of the sample form does not apply, write "Does not apply" in the blank space.

❑ Complete the portions of the sample form with blank spaces. (Do NOT sign just yet.)

❑ If you are using this will for child(ren), but not grandchild(ren), simply put "No" in the blank space for grandchild(ren).

❑ If you are using this will for child(ren) who are NOT minors, then you can simply discard the information for guardianship and the children's trust.

❑ If you do not wish to donate your body or body parts, you can discard this part or simply write in the blank space, "I do NOT want my body, tissues, or any other part of me donated."

❑ Review the will you have completed to ensure all of the form is completed.

❑ Review the State Specific Information at PeerlessLegal.com.

❑ Meet with witnesses.

❑ Meet with Notary Public (if self-proving affidavits is desired).

❑ Double-check the will for completeness and you understand its contents.

❑ Sign and date the will in the presence of witnesses (and notary public if required or desired).

❑ If your will is complicated, or includes numerous additions, then do not use this book for the sole purpose of creating a will. Contact a licensed attorney to create a will that meets you specific needs.

❑ Give a copy of the will to the named executor and to the alternate executor.

❑ Store a record of your final, signed will, in a safe place, along with all of your other important documents that you wish to pass on.

LAST WILL AND TESTAMENT OF

I, _____ DOB: _____,

whose address is _____

located in the County of _____ in the State of _____,

being of sound mind, willfully and voluntarily make this my Last Will and Testament ("WILL").

1. Revocation. I revoke all wills that I have previously made.

2. Marital Status. ❑ Not married ❑ Married to: _____ "SPOUSE"

3. Child(ren). ❑ No (Go to 4.) ❑ Yes, I have _____ number of child(ren):

Name: _____ DOB: _____

Name: _____ DOB: _____

Name: _____ DOB: _____

❑ More child(ren) are listed on a separate added page dated: _____

and titled _____.

Grandchild(ren). ❑ No (Go to 4.) ❑ Yes, I have _____ number of grandchild(ren):

Name: _____ DOB: _____

Name: _____ DOB: _____

Name: _____ DOB: _____

❑ More grandchild(ren) are listed on a separate added page dated: _____

and titled _____.

Omissions of Child(ren) and Grandchild(ren). I do NOT leave property to one or more of the children or grandchildren omitted from the above lists of Child(ren) and Grandchild(ren); my failure to do so is intentional.

_____ My initials confirm that I have read and agreed to this term.

Personal Guardian. If, at the time of my death, any of my children are still minors, and a personal guardian is needed, I name: _____

as the "PERSONAL GUARDIAN," to serve without bond. If they are unable or unwilling to serve as Personal Guardian, I name _____ as Personal Guardian, also to serve without bond.

Property Guardian. If, at the time of my death, any of my children are minors and a property guardian is needed, I name _____

as the "PROPERTY GUARDIAN," to serve without bond. If they are unable or unwilling to serve as Property Guardian, I name _____

as Property Guardian, also to serve without bond.

Children's Trust. Property left in this Will to beneficiaries listed in Section A (below in this Section) is held in a separate trust, administered according to the following terms:

> **A. Trust Beneficiaries and Age Limits.** Each trust ends when the following beneficiaries become 35 years of age, except as otherwise specified in this section.

> Trust Beneficiary (Name)   Trust Ends at Age

> _____   _____

> _____   _____

> _____   _____

> **B. Trustees.** I name _____ "TRUSTEE," to serve without bond. If they are unable or unwilling to serve as Trustee, I name _____ _____ as Trustee, also to serve without bond.

> **C. Beneficiary Provisions.**

> (1) Trustee may distribute for the benefit of each beneficiary as much of the net income or principal of the trust as the Trustee deems necessary for the beneficiary's health, support, maintenance, and education. In deciding whether to make a distribution for or to a beneficiary, the Trustee may take into account the beneficiary's other income, resources, and sources of support.

> (2) Any trust income that is not distributed to a beneficiary by the Trustee will accumulate and will be added to the principal of the trust administered for that beneficiary.

> **D. Termination of Trust.** The trust terminates if and when any of the following occurs:

(A) beneficiary becomes the age specified in Paragraph A of this trust;

(B) beneficiary dies before becoming the age specified in Paragraph A of this trust; or

(C) trust property is used up through distributions allowed under these provisions.

If the trust is terminated due to the beneficiary reaching the age specified in Paragraph A of this trust, the remaining principal and accumulated net income of the trust passes to the trust beneficiary.

If the trust is terminated due to the beneficiary's death, the remaining principal and accumulated net income in the trust passes to the deceased trust beneficiary's heirs.

E. Powers of Trustee. In addition to other powers granted to the Trustee in this Will, the Trustee has the powers:

(1) generally conferred on trustees by the laws of the state having jurisdiction over this trust;

(2) with respect to property in the trust, conferred by this Will on the Executor; and

(3) to hire and pay from trust assets the reasonable fees of investment advisors, accountants, tax advisors, agents, attorneys, and other assistants to administer the trust and manage any trust asset and for any litigation affecting the trust.

F. Trust Administration Provisions.

(1) This trust is to be administered independent of court supervision to the maximum extent possible under the laws of the state having jurisdiction over this trust.

(2) The interests of trust beneficiaries are not transferable by voluntary or involuntary assignment or by operation of law and be free from the claims of creditors and from attachment, execution, bankruptcy or other legal process to the fullest extent permissible by law.

(3) The trustee is entitled to reasonable compensation out of the trust assets for ordinary and extraordinary services, and for all services in connection with the complete or partial termination of any trust created by this Will.

(4) The invalidity of any provision of this trust instrument does not affect the validity of the remaining provisions.

4. Beneficiary Survival Requirement. Beneficiaries named in this Will must survive me by at least thirty (30) calendar days to receive any property under this Will.

5. Simultaneous Death. If any beneficiary and I die simultaneously (in the same transaction and/or occurrence within twenty-nine (29) calendar days from one another), for purposes of this Will, I am presumed to have survived the beneficiary.

6. Define: Survive. In this Will, "survive" means to outlive the will writer by at least forty-five (45) calendar days ("SURVIVE").

7. Specific Gifts. All specific gifts made in this Will to two or more beneficiaries, receive equal interest in the specific gifts, unless unequal shares are specifically indicated. All shared gifts are required to be sold with the net proceeds distributed as directed by this Will, unless all beneficiaries of the gift agree in writing, after the Will creator's death, that the specific gift is not be sold.

If I name two or more primary beneficiaries to receive a specific gift of property and any of the primary beneficiaries does not survive me, then all of the surviving primary beneficiaries receive, in equal shares, the interest in the non-surviving, deceased, primary beneficiary's share (i.e., the last in time surviving, primary beneficiaries take possession of the specific gift with the non-surviving beneficiary's share distributed equally among the remaining, surviving, beneficiaries and no effect on the surviving primary beneficiaries' initial interest), unless I have specifically provided otherwise. If I name two or more alternate beneficiaries to receive a specific gift of property, and any of them do not survive me, all surviving, alternate beneficiaries are to equally divide the deceased, alternate beneficiary's share.

I make the following specific gifts of property that are detailed in **Schedule A**. **Schedule A** is a part of this Will.

8. Residuary Estate. The remaining property not named or disposed of by this Will, or any other manner, including lapsed or failed gifts, is included as part of my residuary estate, which goes:

(My initials are provided next to my **one** selection for the residuary beneficiary of this Will.)

_____ to my Spouse, or if my Spouse does not survive me, alternatively, then to my child(ren): _____, and alternatively, if they do not survive me, then to: _____

_____.

[OR]

_____ to: _____,

and alternatively, if they do not survive me, then to: _____

_____.

If I name two or more alternate residuary beneficiaries to receive property and any of them do not survive me, all surviving alternate residuary beneficiaries are to equally divide the deceased alternate residuary beneficiary's share.

9. Executor. I name _____, "EXECUTOR," to serve

without bond; however, if not qualified, or ceases to serve, then I name _____

_____ as the alternate Executor, who also will serve without bond.

My Executor is directed to take all legal actions to probate this Will, including filing a petition in the proper court for the independent administration of my estate.

The location of all of my documents to be distributed by this Will is: _____

_____.

I grant to my Executor the following powers, to be exercised as the Executor deems in the best interest of my estate, to:

(1) retain property, without liability for loss or depreciation resulting from such retention.

(2) sell, lease, or exchange property and to receive or administer the proceeds as a part of my estate.

(3) vote stock, convert bonds, notes, stocks or other securities belonging to my estate into other securities, and exercise all other rights and privileges of a person owning similar property.

(4) deal with, and settle, claims in favor of or against my estate.

(5) continue, maintain, operate or participate in any business which is a part of my estate, and to incorporate, dissolve or otherwise change the form of organization of the business.

(6) pay all debts and taxes that may be assessed against my estate, as provided under state law.

(7) do all other acts which, in the executor's judgment, may be necessary or appropriate for the proper and advantageous management, investment, and distribution of my estate.

These powers, authority, and discretion are in addition to the powers, authority, and discretion vested in an Executor by operation of law, and may be exercised as often as deemed necessary, without approval by any court in any jurisdiction.

10. Anatomical Gift. I declare, under the Uniform Anatomical Gift Act, to donate to any medical institution willing to accept and use them, and I direct my Executor to carry out such donation of the following body parts and organs: _____

_____

_____

11. Funeral Arrangements. Funeral arrangements have been made with the _____

_____ located at _____

_____

to be buried at _____

located in _____

and I direct my Executor to carry out such arrangements.

I sign my name to this Will this _____ day of _____, 20_____, at

_____, in the State of _____, and declare it is my Will, that I sign willingly, execute freely and voluntarily for the purposes expressed, that I am of the age of majority or otherwise legally empowered to make a Will, and under no constraint or undue influence.

_____   _____
Signature of Testator   Printed Name of Testator

WITNESS STATEMENT

On this _____ day of _____, 20_____, the Testator, _____ declared to us, the undersigned, that this instrument is Testator's Will. Testator requests us to act as witnesses. Testator has signed this Will in our presence, all of us being present at the same time. We now, at the Testator's request, in the Testator's presence, and in the presence of each other, sign and print our names as witnesses to declare that we are of sound mind and of proper age to act as witnesses to a will. We further declare that we understand this to be the Testator's Will, and that, to the best of our knowledge, the Testator is of the legal age, or is otherwise legally empowered to make a will, and appears to be of sound mind and under no constraint or undue influence.

We declare, under penalty of perjury of law, that the above declaration is true and correct, this

_____ day of _____, 20 _____, at _____, located in

the County of _____ in the State of _____.

_____   _____
Witness's Signature   Printed Name of Witness
_____
Address of Witness

_____   _____
Witness's Signature   Printed Name of Witness
_____
Address of Witness

_____   _____
Witness's Signature   Printed Name of Witness
_____
Address of Witness

SCHEDULE A—Specific Gifts.

I make the following specific gifts of property: I leave _____

described as _____

_____

to _____

and, alternatively, if they do not survive me, then to _____

_____

I make the following specific gifts of property: I leave _____

described as _____

_____

to _____

and, alternatively, if they do not survive me, then to _____

_____

I make the following specific gifts of property: I leave _____

described as _____

_____

to _____

and, alternatively, if they do not survive me, then to _____

_____

I make the following specific gifts of property: I leave _____

described as _____

_____

to _____

and, alternatively, if they do not survive me, then to _____

_____

SELF-PROVING AFFIDAVIT 1: Alabama, Alaska, Arizona, Arkansas, Colorado, Connecticut, Hawaii, Idaho, Illinois, Indiana, Maine, Michigan, Minnesota, Mississippi, Montana, Nebraska, Nevada, New Mexico, New York, North Dakota, Oregon, South Carolina, South Dakota, Tennessee, Utah, Virginia, Washington (State), West Virginia, or Wisconsin

We, _____, _____

_____and _____,
the testator and the witnesses, whose names are signed to the attached instrument in those capacities, personally appearing before the undersigned authority and being first duly sworn, declare to the undersigned authority under penalty of perjury that:

(1) the testator declared, signed, and executed the instrument as his or her last will;

(2) he or she signed it willingly or directed another to sign for him or her;

(3) he or she executed it as his or her free and voluntary act for the purposes therein expressed; and

(4) each of the witnesses, at the request of the testator, in his or her hearing and presence and in the presence of each other, signed the will as witnesses, and that to the best of his or her knowledge the testator was at that time of full legal age, of sound mind and under no constraint or undue influence.

Testator's Signature: _____

_____   _____
Witness's Signature   Printed Name of Witness

_____
Address of Witness

_____   _____
Witness's Signature   Printed Name of Witness

_____
Address of Witness

_____   _____
Witness's Signature   Printed Name of Witness

_____
Address of Witness

NOTARY PUBLIC ACKNOWLEDGEMENT

The foregoing instrument was acknowledged, subscribed, and sworn to before me, this _____ day

of _____, 20_____, by _____, the testator, and

by _____, _____,

and _____, personally known to me (or proved to me
on the basis of satisfactory evidence) to be the person whose name is subscribed to the foregoing
instrument, and acknowledged to me that he or she executed the same in his or her authorized
capacity and that by his or her signature on the instrument, the person, or the entity upon behalf
of which the person acted, executed the instrument.

Witness my hand and official seal.

_____

NOTARY PUBLIC for the State of _____

My Commission Expires: _____

[For Notary Seal or Stamp]

_____
NOTARY PUBLIC

SELF-PROVING AFFIDAVIT 2: Delaware, Florida, Georgia, Iowa, Kansas, Kentucky, Massachusetts, Missouri, New Jersey, North Carolina, Oklahoma, Pennsylvania, Rhode Island, or Wyoming

We, _____, _____,

_____and_____

the witnesses, whose names are signed to the attached or foregoing instrument and whose signatures appear below, having appeared together before me and having been first duly sworn, each then declared to me that:

1) the attached or foregoing instrument is the last will of the testator;

2) the testator willingly and voluntarily declared, signed and executed the will in the presence of the witnesses;

3) the witnesses signed the will upon request by the testator, in the presence and hearing of the testator and in the presence of each other;

4) to the best knowledge of each witness the testator was, at that time of the signing, of the age of majority (or otherwise legally competent to make a will), of sound mind and under no constraint or undue influence; and

5) each witness was and is competent, and of the proper age to witness a will.

Testator's Signature: _____

_____   _____
Witness's Signature   Printed Name of Witness

_____
Address of Witness

_____   _____
Witness's Signature   Printed Name of Witness

_____
Address of Witness

_____   _____
Witness's Signature   Printed Name of Witness

_____
Address of Witness

NOTARY PUBLIC ACKNOWLEDGEMENT

The foregoing instrument was acknowledged, subscribed, and sworn to before me, this _____ day

of _____, 20_____, by _____, the testator, and

by _____, _____,

and _____, personally known to me (or proved to me on the basis of satisfactory evidence) to be the person whose name is subscribed to the foregoing instrument, and acknowledged to me that he or she executed the same in his or her authorized capacity and that by his or her signature on the instrument, the person, or the entity upon behalf of which the person acted, executed the instrument.

Witness my hand and official seal.

_____

NOTARY PUBLIC for the State of _____

My Commission Expires: _____

[For Notary Seal or Stamp]

_____

NOTARY PUBLIC

SELF-PROVING AFFIDAVIT TEXAS

THE STATE OF TEXAS, COUNTY OF _____.

Before me, the undersigned authority, on this day personally appeared _____,

_____, _____,

and _____, known to me (or proved to me on the basis of satisfactory evidence) to be the testator and the witnesses, respectively, whose names are subscribed on the foregoing instrument, and, all have been duly sworn by me. The testator declared to me and to the witnesses in my presence that the foregoing instrument is their last will and testament, and that the testator willingly made and executed it as a free act. The witnesses, each on their oath stated to me, in the presence and hearing of the testator, that the testator declared to them that the instrument is the testator's last will and testament, and that the testator executed it and wanted each of them to sign as witnesses. On the witnesses' oaths, each witness stated further that all of the witnesses signed the instrument as witnesses in the presence of the testator at the testator's request, and that the testator was at the time eighteen years of age or over (or being under such age, was or had been lawfully married, or was then a member of the armed forces of the United States or an auxiliary thereof or of the Maritime Service) and was of sound mind, and each witness was then at least fourteen years of age.

Testator's Signature: _____

_____   _____
Witness's Signature   Printed Name of Witness

_____   _____
Witness's Signature   Printed Name of Witness

_____   _____
Witness's Signature   Printed Name of Witness

NOTARY PUBLIC ACKNOWLEDGEMENT

The foregoing instrument was acknowledged, subscribed, and sworn to before me, this _____day of _____, 20_____.

Witness my hand and official seal. _____

NOTARY PUBLIC for the State of _____My Commission Expires: _____

[For Notary Seal or Stamp]

_____
NOTARY PUBLIC

LIVING WILL OF _____

I, _____ (DOB: _____), whose address

is _____ in the County of _____

in the State of _____, ("PRINCIPAL") being of sound mind, willfully, and
voluntarily make this, my Living Will, if I become incompetent or incapacitated to the extent
that I am unable to communicate my wishes, desires, and preferences on my own regarding my
healthcare. This declaration is an expression of my legal right to refuse healthcare and treatment,
and my life is not to be artificially prolonged under the circumstances set forth below, and,
pursuant to any and all applicable laws in the State of _____.

I revoke all Living Wills that I have previously made.

I expect, and trust, all parties involved in my healthcare needs to be legally and morally bound to
act in accordance with my wishes, desires, and preferences in this document. I declare:

(By placing my initials before each number means I grant those powers, and where there are no
initials means I do NOT grant those powers. I may also cross out powers which are NOT
granted. Where there are letters as subparts to the numbers, I place my initials next to the
numbers and letters to confirm the grant of the specific powers. Each of the letters that have been
agreed to, are initialed. No initial next to a letter, means the power is not granted to that part.)

_____ 1. **Terminal Condition.** If I should have an incurable or irreversible condition
which has been certified as a terminal condition that will cause my death within a
relatively short time by my attending physician and one additional physician, both
of whom have personally examined me, and such physicians have determined that
there can be no recovery from such condition and my death is imminent, and
where the application of life prolonging procedures would serve only to
artificially prolong the dying process, and are not necessary to my comfort, care,
or to alleviate pain, then this authorization includes, but is not limited to, the
withholding or the withdrawal of the following types of medical treatment
(subject to any special instructions in Paragraph 7 below):

_____ a. Artificial feeding and hydration.

_____ b. Cardiopulmonary resuscitation (this includes, but is not limited to,
the use of drugs, electric shock, and artificial breathing).

_____ c. Kidney dialysis.

_____ d. Surgery or other invasive procedures.

_____ e. Drugs and antibiotics.

_____ f. Transfusions of blood or blood products.

_____ g. Other: _____

_____.

_____ 2. **Irreversible Coma or Persistent Vegetative State.** If I should be in an irreversible coma or persistent vegetative state which has been certified as incurable by my attending physician and one additional physician, both of whom have personally examined me, and such physicians have determined that there can be no recovery from such condition and my death is imminent, and where the application of life prolonging procedures would serve only to artificially prolong the dying process, and are not necessary to my comfort, care, or to alleviate pain, then this authorization includes, but is not limited to, the **withholding or the withdrawal of the following types of medical treatment** (subject to any special instructions in Paragraph 7 below):

_____ a. Artificial feeding and hydration.

_____ b. Cardiopulmonary resuscitation (this includes, but is not limited to, the use of drugs, electric shock, and artificial breathing).

_____ c. Kidney dialysis.

_____ d. Surgery or other invasive procedures.

_____ e. Drugs and antibiotics.

_____ f. Transfusions of blood or blood products.

_____ g. Other: _____

_____.

_____ 3. **Medical Condition Where I Cannot Communicate.** If I have a medical condition where I am unable to communicate my desires as to treatment, and my physician determines that the burdens of treatment outweigh the expected benefits, I direct my attending physician to withhold or withdraw medical procedures and treatment other than the medical procedures and treatment necessary for my comfort or to alleviate pain. This authorization includes, but is not limited to, the **withholding or withdrawal of the following types of medical treatment** (subject to any special instructions in paragraph 7 below):

_____ a. Artificial feeding and hydration.

_____ b. Cardiopulmonary resuscitation (this includes, but is not limited to, the use of drugs, electric shock, and artificial breathing).

_____ c. Kidney dialysis.

_____ d. Surgery or other invasive procedures.

_____ e. Drugs and antibiotics.

_____ f. Transfusions of blood or blood products.

_____ g. Other: _____

_____.

_____ 4. **Life Prolonged.** I want my life prolonged to the greatest extent possible (subject to any special instructions in paragraph 7 below).

_____ 5. **Pregnancy.** If I am diagnosed as pregnant, this document shall have no force and effect during my pregnancy.

_____ 6. **Durable Power of Attorney for Healthcare.** If I have also signed a Durable Power of Attorney for Healthcare, Appointment of Healthcare Agent, or Healthcare Proxy, I direct the person who I have appointed with such instrument to follow the directions that I have made in this document.

_____ 7. **Additional Directions.** I have the following additional directions: _____

_____

_____.

_____ 8. **Limitations on Decision-Makers.** I DO NOT want the following person(s) to be involved in any manner in the decision-making regarding my medical treatment, or the withholding or withdrawal of medical treatment: _____

_____

_____.

I understand the full importance of this declaration, and I am emotionally and mentally competent to make this declaration and Living Will. I also understand that I may revoke this document at any time. I publish and sign this Living Will on this ____ day of _____, 20____, and declare that I do so freely, for the purposes expressed, under no constraint or undue influence, and that I am of sound mind and of legal age.

Principal's Signature: _____

WITNESS STATEMENT

On this _____day of _____, 20_____, the Principal, _____

_____ declared to us, the undersigned, that this instrument is the Principal's Living Will. Principal has signed this Living Will in our presence, all of us being present at the same time. We now, at the Principal's request, in the Principal's presence, and in the presence of each other, sign and print our names as witnesses to declare that we are of sound mind and of proper age to act as witnesses to a living will. We further declare that to the best of our knowledge the Principal is of the legal age, or is otherwise legally empowered to make a living will, and appears to be of sound mind and under no constraint or undue influence. We are not the Principal's attending physician, or a patient or employee of the Principal's attending physi-cian; or a patient, physician, or employee of the healthcare facility in which the Principal is a patient, unless such person is required or allowed to witness the execution of this document by the laws of the state in which this document is executed. We also are not entitled to any portion of the Principal's estate on the Principal's death under the laws of intestate succession of any state, or under the Last Will and Testament of the Principal or any Codicil to such Last Will and Testament, and not directly financially responsible for the Principal's medical care. We further did not sign the Principal's signature for the Principal or on the direction of the Principal, nor have we been paid any fee for acting as witnesses to the execution of this document.

We declare, under penalty of perjury of law, that the above declaration is true and correct, this

_____day of _____, 20 _____, at _____, located in

the County of _____in the State of _____.

_____   _____
Witness's Signature   Printed Name of Witness
_____
Address of Witness

_____   _____
Witness's Signature   Printed Name of Witness
_____
Address of Witness

_____   _____
Witness's Signature   Printed Name of Witness
_____
Address of Witness

NOTARY PUBLIC ACKNOWLEDGEMENT

The foregoing instrument was acknowledged, subscribed, and sworn to before me, this ____day

of _____, 20_____, by _____, the Principal,

and by _____, _____,

and _____, personally known to me (or proved to me on the basis of satisfactory evidence) to be the person whose name is subscribed to the foregoing instrument, and acknowledged to me that he or she executed the same in his or her authorized capacity and that by his or her signature on the instrument, the person, or the entity upon behalf of which the person acted, executed the instrument.

Witness my hand and official seal.

_____

NOTARY PUBLIC for the State of _____

My Commission Expires: _____

[For Notary Seal or Stamp]

_____

NOTARY PUBLIC

WILL AMENDMENT

I, _____(DOB:_____), whose address

is _____in the County of _____

in the State of _____, declare that this is an amendment to my Will that is dated:

_____.

1) I make the following changes: _____

_____

_____

_____

_____

_____

_____

2) I add the following to my Will: _____

_____

_____

_____

_____

_____

_____

_____

3) In all other respects, I confirm and republish my Will dated _____
as modified by this amendment.

I subscribe my name to this amendment this day of _____, 20____, at _____, located in the County of _____ in the State of _____

and I declare, under penalty of perjury of the law, that I am signing and executing this amendment willingly, under my own free and voluntary act, and that I am of the age of majority or otherwise legally empowered to make an amendment, and I am under no constraint or undue influence.

_____
Signature

WITNESS STATEMENT

On this _____ day of _____, 20_____, the Testator, _____, declared to us, the undersigned, that this instrument is Testator's amendment. Testator requests us to act as witnesses. Testator has signed this amendment in our presence, all of us being present at the same time. We now, at the Testator's request, in the Testator's presence, and in the presence of each other, sign and print our names as witnesses to declare that we are of sound mind and of proper age to act as witnesses to an amendment to a will. We further declare that we understand this to be the Testator's amendment, and that to the best of our knowledge the Testator is of the legal age, or is otherwise legally empowered to make an amendment and will, and appears to be of sound mind and under no constraint or undue influence.

We declare, under penalty of perjury of law, that the above declaration is true and correct, this

_____ day of _____, 20_____, at _____, located in

the County of _____ in the State of _____.

_____   _____
Witness's Signature   Printed Name of Witness
_____
Address of Witness

_____   _____
Witness's Signature   Printed Name of Witness
_____
Address of Witness

_____   _____
Witness's Signature   Printed Name of Witness
_____
Address of Witness

WILL REVOCATION

I, _____ (DOB:_____), whose address

is _____ in the County of _____

in the State of _____, revoke the my Will dated: _____, and

titled _____ in its entirety without

limitations, including revoking any appointment of any persons named in the above Will.

Revoking party's signature: _____ Date: _____

NOTARY PUBLIC ACKNOWLEDGEMENT

The foregoing instrument was acknowledged, subscribed, and sworn to before me,

_____ this _____ day of _____,

20____, personally known to me (or proved to me on the basis of satisfactory evidence) to be the person whose name is subscribed to the foregoing instrument, and acknowledged to me that he or she executed the same in his or her authorized capacity and that by his or her signature on the instrument, the person, or the entity upon behalf of which the person acted, executed the instrument.

Witness my hand and official seal.

NOTARY PUBLIC for the State of _____, County of _____

My Commission Expires: _____

[For Notary Seal or Stamp]

Ethical Will

From: _____

_____

_____

Date: _____

To: _____

_____

_____

I write this letter, my ethical will, to you now, in the hopes that in reading this will provide you strength, and the chance to remember me. In creating this ethical will, I share with you some wisdom I have acquired over my life about love, happiness, and my dreams. I hope you will feel my love for you through this letter.

First, I love you! _____

_____

_____

I believe that we never truly loose the people we love. _____

_____

_____

The message I leave to you is that I have lived, loved, and found peace. _____

_____

_____

I have lived. _____

_____

_____

I have loved. _____

_____

_____

I have found peace. _____

_____

_____

What I value: _____

_____

What I believe in: _____

_____

Lessons I have learned. _____

_____

_____

You have meant so much to me. _____

_____

I leave you with these thoughts. _____

_____

_____

My last wishes are: _____

_____

_____

We will see each other again. _____

_____

My final thoughts are with you. _____

_____

Love: _____

Explanation Letter

From: _____

_____

_____

Date: _____

To: _____

_____

_____

I write this letter, in order to provide you with some explanation and clarity for why I have made certain decisions in my will. I hope this will help to avoid any prolonged disputes about the contents of my will and estate.

I intentionally left unequal shares of: _____.

By doing this, I hope to achieve: _____

_____.

I intentionally left unequal shares of: _____.

By doing this, I hope to achieve: _____

_____.

I intentionally left unequal shares of: _____.

By doing this, I hope to achieve: _____

_____.

I intentionally left unequal shares of: _____.

By doing this, I hope to achieve: _____

_____.

Signature: _____   Date: _____

2. Power of Attorney

Power of Attorney Checklist

❑ Make additional copies of any specific pages you may need or tear them out of the book.

❑ Read over the blank form.

❑ If there are parts of the form you do not understand, read the applicable section within this book.

❑ Make adjustments to the form to meet your needs. If the paragraph or portion of the sample form does not apply, write "Does not apply" in the blank space.

❑ Complete the portions of the sample form with blank spaces. (Do NOT sign just yet.)

❑ Review the Power of Attorney you have completed to ensure all of the form is completed.

❑ Review the State Specific Information at PeerlessLegal.com.

❑ Meet with witnesses and with the Notary Public.

❑ Make sure that you the information you have provided is complete and that you understand what is contained within the Power of Attorney.

❑ Sign and date the Power of Attorney in the presence of the witnesses and Notary Public.

❑ If your Power of Attorney is complicated or includes numerous additions, then do not use this book or its contents for the sole purpose of creating a Power of Attorney. Contact a licensed attorney to help you create a Power of Attorney that meets your specific needs.

❑ Give a copy of the complete Power of Attorney to the named Agent and to the alternative Agent.

❑ Store the completed Power of Attorney in a safe place, along with all other important documents that you wish to pass on.

DURABLE POWER OF ATTORNEY FOR HEALTHCARE

I, _____ (DOB: _____) whose address

is _____ in the County of _____

in the State of _____, appoint _____,

who resides at _____

as my agent for healthcare and related personal decisions for me except as I provide otherwise in this document ("AGENT"). If my Agent is unable or unwilling to make those decisions, I appoint as an alternate Agent _____, residing

at _____.

I grant my Agent the maximum power allowed under the law to perform any acts, or make any decisions, on my behalf regarding healthcare matters that I could do, or make, personally, under the laws of the State of _____, including making healthcare decisions on my behalf under the terms and conditions set forth below. My Agent accepts this appointment and agrees to act in my best interest as my Agent considers advisable. This Durable Power of Attorney for Healthcare may be revoked, by me, at any time, and is automatically revoked upon my death.

I revoke all Durable Power of Attorney for Healthcare that I have previously made.

I specifically DO NOT want the following person(s) to be involved, in any manner, in the decision-making regarding my medical treatment, or the withholding or withdrawal of medical treatment: _____

_____.

This Durable Power of Attorney for Healthcare has the following terms and conditions:

1. Superior Document. If I have signed a Living Will or a Directive to Physicians that is valid, then I direct my Agent to follow the directions set out in that document.

2. Terminal Condition Diagnosis. If, at any time, I am diagnosed as having an incurable injury, disease, or illness, which has been certified as a terminal condition by my attending physician and one additional physician, both of which have personally examined me, and such physicians have determined that there can be no recovery from such a condition, and where the application of life prolonging procedures would only serve to artificially prolong the dying process, then:

>   I direct my Agent to withhold or withdraw such procedures, and that I may be permitted to die naturally, with only the administration of medication, the administration of

nutrition and/or hydration, or the performance of any medical procedure deemed necessary to provide comfort, care, or to alleviate pain.

3. Persistent Vegetative State Diagnosis. If, at any time, I am diagnosed as being in a persistent, vegetative state, which has been certi-fied as incurable by my attending physician and one additional physician after both have personally examined me, and such physicians have determined that there can be no recovery from such a condition, and where the application of life prolonging procedures would serve only to artificially prolong the dying process, then:

I direct that my Agent should withhold or withdraw such procedures, and that I be permitted to die naturally with only the administration of medication, the administration of nutrition and/or hydration, or the performance of any medical procedure deemed necessary to provide me with comfort, care, or to alleviate pain.

4. Effective Date and Durability. My Agent may only act if I am unable to participate in making decisions regarding my medical treatment. My attending physician and another physician or licensed psychologist must determine, after examining me, whether I am unable to participate in making my own medical decisions. This designation is suspended during any period when I regain the ability to participate in my own medical treatment decisions. I intend this document to be a Durable Power of Attorney for Healthcare and to survive my disability or incapacity. If I am able to communicate in any manner, including even blinking my eyes, I direct that my healthcare representative try and discuss with me the specifics of any proposed healthcare decision.

5. Agent's Powers. I grant my Agent full authority to make decisions for me. In making such decisions, the Agent must follow my expressed wishes, either written or oral, regarding my medical treatment. If my Agent cannot determine the choice I would want, based on my written or oral statements, then my Agent is to choose for me based on what my Agent believes to be in my best interest. I direct that my Agent comply with the following instructions or limitations:

_____

_____

_____.

I have discussed my healthcare wishes with my Agent and I am satisfied that my Agent knows my wishes with respect to my healthcare and I have full faith and confidence in their judgment. I further direct that my Agent have full authority to do the following, should I lack the capacity to make such a decision myself, provided, however, that this listing is construed in no way to limit the full authority I give my Agent to make healthcare decisions on my behalf to:

a. give informed consent to any healthcare procedure;

b. sign documents necessary to carry out, or withhold, any healthcare procedures on my behalf, including any waivers or releases of liabilities required by any healthcare provider;

c. give or withhold consent for any healthcare or treatment;

d. revoke or change any consent previously given, or implied by law for any healthcare treatment;

e. arrange for, or authorize, my placement or removal from any healthcare facility or institution;

f. require any procedures be discontinued; including the withholding of any medical treatment and/or aid, including nutrition, hydration, and any other medical procedure deemed necessary to provide comfort, care, or to alleviate pain, subject to the conditions previously provided in this docu-ment;

g. authorize the administration of pain-relieving drugs, even if they may shorten my life.

I wish for all my healthcare matters to be carried out through the authority that I have provided to my Agent in this document, despite any contrary wishes, beliefs, or opinions of any members of my family, relatives, or friends.

6. Life-Sustaining Treatment. (CHOOSE <u>ONLY</u> ONE OR NONE of the three.) I understand that I do not have to choose any of the instructions regarding life-sustaining treatment listed below. If I choose one, I will place a mark by the choice and sign below my choice. If I sign one of the choices listed below, I direct that reasonable measures be taken to keep me comfortable and to relieve pain.

❑   <u>CHOICE 1</u>: Life-sustaining treatment: I grant discretion to my Agent.

I do not want life-sustaining treatment (❑ including artificial delivery of food and water ❑ except for artificial delivery of food and water) if any of the following medical conditions exist:

a. I am in an irreversible coma or persistent vegetative state.

b. I am terminally ill, and life-sustaining procedures would only serve to artificially delay my death.

c. My medical condition is such that the burdens of treatment outweigh the expected benefits. In making this determination, I want my Patient Advocate to consider relief of my suffering, the expenses involved, and the quality of life, if prolonged.

I expressly authorize my Agent to make decisions to withhold or withdraw treatment which would allow me to die, and I acknowledge such decisions could or would result in my death.

Signed: _____

[OR]

❑   CHOICE 2: Life-sustaining treatment: I authorize my Agent to withhold all medical treatment if I am ever in a coma or in a persistent, vegetative state.

I want life-sustaining treatment (❑ including artificial delivery of food and water ❑ except for artificial delivery of food and water) unless I am in a coma or persistent vegetative state that my physician reasonably believes to be irreversible. Once my physician has reasonably concluded that I will remain unconscious for the rest of my life, I do not want life-sustaining treatment to be provided or continued.

I expressly authorize my Agent to make decisions to withhold or withdraw treatment which would allow me to die, and I acknowledge such decisions could or would result in my death.

Signed: _____

[OR]

❑   CHOICE 3: Directive for maximum treatment.

I want my life to be prolonged to the greatest extent possible consistent with sound medical practice without regard to my condition, the chances I have for recovery, or the cost of the procedures, and I direct life-sustaining treatment to be provided in order to prolong my life.

Signed: _____

7. If No Agent. If I am unable to participate in making decisions for my care, and there is no Agent to act for me, I request for the instructions I have given in this document to be followed and that those instructions will be considered conclusive evidence of my wishes.

8. Administrative Provisions. I revoke any prior durable powers of attorney for healthcare that I may have executed to the extent that they grant powers and authority within the scope of the powers granted to the Agent appointed in this document.

Photocopies of this signed, power of attorney shall be treated as original counterparts.

9. Duration. This Durable Power of Attorney for Healthcare exists, indefinitely, from its date of execution, until I revoke it.

I am providing these instructions voluntarily, I am at least eighteen years old, and of sound mind.

Date: _____ Signature: _____

WITNESS STATEMENT

On this _____ day of _____, 20_____, we, _____

and _____, declare under penalty of perjury that the person who signed or acknowledged this document is personally known to me (or proved to me on the basis of convincing evidence) to be the principal, that the principal signed or acknowledged this durable power of attorney for healthcare in my presence, that the principal appears to be of sound mind and under no duress, fraud, or undue influence. We are not appointed as Agent by this document. We are not related to the principal by blood, marriage, or adoption. We would not be entitled to any portion of the principal's estate upon the principal's death. We are not the attending physician of the principal or an employee of the attending physician. We have no claim against any portion of the principal's estate upon the principal's death. Furthermore, if we are an employee of a healthcare facility in which the principal is a patient, we are not involved in providing direct patient care to the principal and not one of us is an officer, director, partner, or business office employee of the healthcare facility or of any parent organization of the healthcare facility.

_____   _____
Witness's Signature   Printed Name of Witness
_____
Address of Witness

_____   _____
Witness's Signature   Printed Name of Witness
_____
Address of Witness

NOTARY PUBLIC ACKNOWLEDGEMENT

The foregoing instrument was acknowledged, subscribed, and sworn to before me, this _____day

of _____, 20_____, by _____, and witnessed

by _____, and _____,
personally known to me (or proved to me on the basis of satisfactory evidence) to be the person
whose name is subscribed to the foregoing instrument, and acknowledged to me that he or she
executed the same in his or her authorized capacity and that by his or her signature on the
instrument, the person, or the entity upon behalf of which the person acted, executed the
instrument.

Witness my hand and official seal.

_____

NOTARY PUBLIC for the State of _____

My Commission Expires: _____

[For Notary Seal or Stamp]

_____

NOTARY PUBLIC

FINANCIAL DURABLE POWER OF ATTORNEY

I, _____(DOB: _____), whose address

is _____in the County of _____

in the State of _____,"PRINCIPAL," appoint _____,

whose address is_____

as my Power of Attorney for financial and related decisions for me, except as I provide otherwise in this document ("AGENT"). If my Agent is unable or unwilling to make those decisions, I

appoint, as an alternate Agent, _____, whose address

is _____.

I grant my Agent the maximum power allowed under the law to perform any acts on my behalf regarding financial matters that I could do personally under the laws of the State of _____ _____, on my behalf under the terms and conditions below. My Agent will act as my attorney-in-fact to act in my name, place, and stead in any way which I myself could do with respect to the matters in this document, to the extent that I am permitted by law to act through an Agent. My Agent accepts this appointment and agrees to act in my best interest as my Agent considers advisable.

By placing my initials before one selection below means I grant those powers of attorney to my Agent. Where there are no initials means I do NOT grant those powers of attorney to my Agent.

_____ **THIS FINANCIAL DURABLE POWER OF ATTORNEY IS EFFECTIVE IMMEDIATELY.**

[OR]

_____ **THIS FINANCIAL DURABLE POWER OF ATTORNEY IS ONLY EFFECTIVE IF I BECOME PERMANENTLY DISABILITY OR INCAPACITATED, WHICH HAS BEEN CERTIFIED AS INCURABLE BY MY ATTENDING PHYSICIAN AND ONE ADDITIONAL PHYSICAN, BOTH OF WHOM HAVE PERSONALLY EXAMINED ME, AND SUCH PHYSICIANS HAVE DETERMINED THAT THERE CAN BE NO RECOVERY FROM SUCH CONDITION AND MY DEATH IS IMMINENT, AND I AM THEREFORE UNABLE TO MAKE MY OWN HEALTHCARE DECISIONS.**

I revoke all Financial Durable Power of Attorneys that I have previously made.

This document may be revoked by me at any time, and is automatically revoked upon my death (or if I regain the ability to make my own decisions should the Power of Attorney be effective only if I become incapacitated). By placing my initials before each item below, I grant those powers of attorney to my Agent, and where there are no initials, that means that I do NOT grant those powers of attorney to my Agent. I may also cross out any powers which I do NOT wish to grant.

_____ **A. Real Estate Transactions.** The Principal authorizes the Agent to: (1) demand, receive, and obtain, by litigation or otherwise, money or other things of value to which the Principal is, may become, or claims to be entitled, and conserve, invest, disburse, or use anything so received for the purposes intended; (2) contract in any manner with any person, on terms agreeable to the Agent, to accomplish a purpose of a transaction, and perform, rescind, reform, release, or modify the contract or another contract made by or on behalf of the Principal; (3) execute, acknowledge, seal, and deliver a deed, revocation, mortgage, security agreement, lease, notice, check, promissory note, electronic funds transfer, release, or other instrument or communication the Agent considers appropriate to accomplish a purpose of a transaction; (4) prosecute, defend, submit to arbitration or mediation, settle, or propose or accept a compromise with respect to an existing claim in favor of or against the Principal or intervene in litigation relating to the claim; (5) seek on the Principal's behalf the assistance of a court to carry out an act authorized by the Principal in this Power of Attorney; (6) engage, compensate, and discharge an attorney, accountant, expert witness, or other assistant; (7) keep appropriate records of each transaction, including an accounting of receipts and disbursements; (8) prepare, execute, and file a record, report, or other document the Agent considers desirable to safeguard or promote the Principal's interest under a statute or governmental regulation; (9) reimburse the Agent for expenditures properly made by the Agent in exercising the powers granted by this Power of Attorney; and (10) in general, do any other lawful act with respect to the power and all property related to the power.

_____ **B. Tangible Personal Property.** The Principal authorizes the Agent to: (1) accept as a gift or as security for an extension of credit, reject, demand, buy, receive, or otherwise acquire ownership or possession of tangible, personal property or an interest in tangible, personal property; (2) sell, exchange, convey, with or without covenants, release, surrender, create a security interest in, grant options concerning, lease, sublease to others, or otherwise dispose of tangible, personal property or an interest in tangible, personal property; (3) release, assign, satisfy, or enforce by litigation or otherwise, a security interest, lien, or other claim on behalf of the Principal, with respect to tangible, personal property or an interest in tangible, personal property; (4) manage or conserve tangible, personal property or an interest in tangible, personal property on behalf of the Principal, including: (a) insuring against casualty, liability, or loss; (b) obtaining or regaining possession, or protecting the property or interest, by litigation or otherwise; (c) paying, compromising, or contesting taxes or assessments or applying for and receiving refunds in connection with taxes or assessments; (d) moving from place to place; (e) storing for hire or on a gratuitous bailment; and (f) using, altering, and making repairs or alterations; and (5) change the form of title of an interest in tangible, personal property.

C. Stocks and Bonds. The Principal authorizes the Agent to: (1) buy, sell, and exchange stocks, bonds, mutual funds, and all other types of securities and financial instruments, whether held directly or indirectly, except commodity futures contracts and call and put options on stocks and stock indexes, (2) receive certificates and other evidences of ownership with respect to securities, (3) exercise voting rights with respect to securities in person or by proxy, enter into voting trusts, and consent to limitations on the right to vote.

D. Commodity and Options Transactions. The Principal authorizes the Agent to: (1) buy, sell, exchange, assign, settle, and exercise commodity futures contracts and call and put options on stocks and stock indexes traded on a regulated option exchange, and (2) establish, continue, modify, and terminate option accounts with a broker.

E. Banking (and Other Related Financial Institutions) Transactions. The Principal authorizes the Agent to: (1) continue, modify, and terminate an account or other banking arrangement made by, or on behalf of, the Principal; (2) establish, modify, and terminate an account or other banking arrangement with a bank, trust company, savings and loan association, credit union, thrift company, brokerage firm, or other financial institution selected by the Agent; (3) rent a safe deposit box or space in a vault; (4) contract for other services available from a financial institution as the Agent considers desirable; (5) withdraw by check, order, or otherwise money or property of the Principal deposited with, or left in, the custody of a financial institution; 6) receive bank statements, vouchers, notices, and similar documents from a financial institution and act with respect to them; (7) enter a safe deposit box or vault and withdraw or add to the contents; (8) borrow money at an interest rate agreeable to the Agent and pledge personal property of the Principal as security, when necessary, in order to borrow, pay, renew, or extend the time of payment of a debt of the Principal; (9) make, assign, draw, endorse, discount, guarantee, and negotiate promissory notes, checks, drafts, and other negotiable or nonnegotiable paper of the Principal, or payable to the Principal or the Principal's order, transfer money, receive the cash or other proceeds of those transactions, accept a draft drawn by a person upon the

Principal, and pay it when due; (10) receive for the Principal and act upon a sight draft, warehouse receipt, or other negotiable or nonnegotiable instrument; (11) apply for, receive, and use letters of credit, credit and debit cards, and traveler's checks from a financial institution and give an indemnity or other agreement in connection with letters of credit; and (12) consent to an extension of the time of payment with respect to commercial paper or a financial transaction with a financial institution.

_____

F. Business Operating Transactions. The Principal authorizes the Agent to: (1) operate, buy, sell, enlarge, reduce, and terminate business interests; (2) act for a Principal, subject to the terms of a partnership agreement or operating agreement, to: (a) perform a duty or discharge a liability and exercise a right, power, privilege, or option that the Principal has, may have, or claims to have, under the partnership agreement or operating agreement, whether or not the Principal is a partner in a partnership or member of a limited liability company; (b) enforce the terms of any partnership agreement or operating agreement by litigation or otherwise; and (c) defend, submit to arbitration, settle, or compromise litigation to which the Principal is a party because of membership in a partnership or limited liability company; (3) exercise in person or by proxy, or enforce by litigation or otherwise, a right, power, privilege, or option the Principal has or claims to have as the holder of a bond, share, or other instrument of similar character and defend, submit to arbitration or mediation, settle, or compromise litigation to which the Principal is a party because of a bond, share, or similar instrument; (4) with respect to a business controlled by the Principal: (a) continue, modify, renegotiate, extend, and terminate a contract made by or on behalf of the Principal with respect to the business before execution of the Power of Attorney; (b) determine: (i) the location of its operation; (ii) the nature and extent of its business; (iii) the methods of manufacturing, selling, merchandising, financing, accounting, and advertising employed in its operation; (iv) the amount and types of insurance carried; and (v) the mode of engaging, compensating, and dealing with its accountants, attorneys, other Agents, and employees; (c) change the name or form of organization under which the business is operated and enter into a partnership agreement or operating agreement with other persons or organize a corporation or other business entity to take over all or part of the operation of the business; and (d) demand and receive money due or claimed by the Principal or on the Principal's behalf in the operation of the business, and control and disburse the money in the operation of the business; (5) put additional capital into a business in which the Principal has an interest; (6) join in a plan of reorganization, consolidation, or merger of the business; (7) sell or liquidate a business or part of it at the time and upon the terms the Agent considers desirable; (8) establish the value of a business under a buy-out agreement to which the Principal is a party;

(9) prepare, sign, file, and deliver reports, compilations of information, returns, or other papers with respect to a business which are required by a governmental agency or instrumentality or which the Agent considers desirable, and make related payments; and (10) pay, compromise, or contest taxes or assessments and perform any other act that the Agent considers desirable to protect the Principal from illegal or unnecessary taxation, fines, penalties, or assessments with respect to a business, including attempts to recover, in any manner permitted by law, money paid before or after the execution of this Power of Attorney.

_____

G. Insurance and Annuities. The Principal authorizes the Agent to: (1) continue, pay the premium or assessment on, modify, rescind, release, or terminate a contract procured by or on behalf of the Principal which insures or provides an annuity to either the Principal or another person, whether or not the Principal is a beneficiary under the contract; (2) procure new, different, and additional contracts of insurance and annuities for the Principal and the Principal's spouse, children, and other dependents, and select the amount, type of insurance or annuity, and mode of payment; (3) pay the premium or assessment on, modify, rescind, release, or terminate a contract of insurance or annuity procured by the Agent; (4) apply for and receive a loan on the security of a contract of insurance or annuity; (5) surrender and receive the cash surrender value; (6) exercise an election; (7) change the manner of paying premiums; (8) change or convert the type of insurance or annuity, with respect to which the Principal has or claims to have a power described in this section; (9) apply for and procure government aid to guarantee or pay premiums of a contract of insurance on the life of the Principal; (10) collect, sell, assign, hypothecate, borrow upon, or pledge the interest of the Principal in a contract of insurance or annuity; and (11) pay from proceeds or otherwise, compromise or contest, and apply for refunds in connection with, a tax or assessment levied by a taxing authority with respect to a contract of insurance or annuity or its proceeds or liability accruing by reason of the tax or assessment.

_____

H. Estate Transactions (Including Trusts and Other Transactions Where Principal is Beneficiary). The Principal authorizes the Agent to act for the Principal in all matters that affect a trust, probate estate, guardianship, conservatorship, escrow, custodianship, or other fund from which the Principal is, may become, or claims to be entitled, as a beneficiary, to a share or payment, including to: (1) accept, reject, disclaim, receive, receipt for, sell, assign, release, pledge, exchange, or consent to a reduction in or modification of a share in or payment from the fund; (2) demand or obtain by litigation or otherwise money or other thing of value to which the Principal is, may become, or claims to be entitled by reason of the fund; (3) initiate, participate in, and oppose litigation to ascertain the meaning, validity, or effect of a deed, will, declaration of trust, or other instrument or transaction affecting the interest of the Principal; (4) initiate, participate in, and oppose litigation to remove, substitute, or surcharge a fiduciary; (5) conserve, invest, disburse, and use anything received for an authorized purpose; and (6) transfer an interest of the Principal in real property, stocks, bonds, accounts with financial institutions or securities intermediaries, insurance, annuities, and other property, to the trustee of a revocable trust created by the Principal as settlor.

_____ **I. Claims and Litigation.** The Principal authorizes the Agent to: (1) assert and prosecute before a court or administrative agency a claim, a claim for relief, cause of action, counterclaim, offset, or defense against an individual, organization, or government, including actions to recover property or other thing of value, to recover damages sustained by the Principal, to eliminate or modify tax liability, or to seek an injunction, specific performance, or other relief; (2) bring an action to determine adverse claims, intervene in litigation, and act as amicus curiae; (3) in connection with litigation, procure an attachment, garnishment, libel, order of arrest, or other preliminary, provisional, or intermediate relief and use an available procedure to effect or satisfy a judgment, order, or decree; (4) in connection with litigation, perform any lawful act, including acceptance of tender, offer of judgment, admission of facts, submission of a controversy on an agreed statement of facts, consent to examination before trial, and binding the Principal in litigation; (5) submit to arbitration or mediation, settle, and propose or accept a compromise with respect to a claim or litigation; (6) waive the issuance and service of process upon the Principal, accept service of process, appear for the Principal, designate persons upon whom process directed to the Principal may be served, execute and file or deliver stipulations on the Principal's behalf, verify pleadings, seek appellate review, procure and give surety and indemnity bonds, contract and pay for the preparation and printing of records and briefs, receive and execute and file or deliver a consent, waiver, release, confession of judgment, satisfaction of judgment, notice, agreement, or other instrument in connection with the prosecution, settlement, or defense of a claim or litigation; (7) act for the Principal with respect to bankruptcy or insolvency, whether voluntary or involuntary, concerning the Principal or some other person, or with respect to a reorganization, receivership, or application for the appointment of a receiver or trustee which affects an interest of the Principal in property or other thing of value; and (8) pay a judgment against the Principal or a settlement made in connection with litigation and receive and conserve money or other thing of value paid in settlement of or as proceeds of a claim or litigation.

_____ **J. Personal and Family Maintenance.** The Principal authorizes the Agent to: (1) perform the acts necessary to maintain the customary standard of living of the

Principal, the Principal's spouse, children, and other individuals customarily or legally entitled to be supported by the Principal, including providing living quarters by purchase, lease, or other contract, or paying the operating costs, including interest, amortization payments, repairs, and taxes, on premises owned by the Principal and occupied by those individuals; (2) provide for the individuals described under (1) normal domestic help, usual vacations and travel expenses, and funds for shelter, clothing, food, appropriate education, and other current living costs; (3) pay on behalf of the individuals described under (1) expenses for necessary medical, dental, and surgical care, hospitalization, and custodial care; (4) act as the Principal's personal representative pursuant to the Social Security Act, and applicable regulations, in making decisions related to the past, present, or future payment for the provision of healthcare consented to by the Principal or anyone authorized under the law of this state to consent to healthcare on behalf of the Principal; (5) continue any provision made by the Principal, for the individuals described under (1), for automobiles or other means of transportation, including registering, licensing, insuring, and replacing them; (6) maintain or open charge accounts for the convenience of the individuals described under (1) and open new accounts the Agent considers desirable to accomplish a lawful purpose; and (7) continue payments incidental to the membership or affiliation of the Principal in a church, club, society, order, or other organization or to continue contributions to those organizations.

_____

K. Benefits From Social Security, Medicare, Medicaid, Military Service, Other Government Programs. The Principal authorizes the Agent to: (1) execute vouchers in the name of the Principal for allowances and reimbursements payable by the United States or a foreign government or by a state or subdivision of a state to the Principal, including allowances and reimbursements for transportation of the individuals, and for shipment of their household effects; (2) take possession and order the removal and shipment of property of the Principal from a post, warehouse, depot, dock, or other place of storage or safekeeping, either governmental or private, and execute and deliver a release, voucher, receipt, bill of lading, shipping ticket, certificate, or other instrument for that purpose; (3) prepare, file, and prosecute a claim of the Principal to a benefit or assistance, financial or otherwise, to which the Principal claims to be entitled under a statute or governmental regulation; (4) prosecute, defend, submit to arbitration or mediation, settle, and propose or accept a compromise with respect to any benefit or assistance the Principal may be entitled to receive under a statute or governmental regulation; and (5) receive the financial proceeds of a claims and conserve, invest, disburse, or use anything so received for a lawful purpose. I intend for my attorney-in-fact under this Power of Attorney to be treated as I would be with respect to my rights regarding the use and disclosure of my individually identifiable health information or other medical records. This release authority applies to any information governed by the Health Insurance Portability and Accountability Act of 1996 (a.k.a. HIPAA).

_____ **L. Records, Reports and Statements.** The Principal authorizes the Agent to: (1) demand, receive, and obtain by litigation or otherwise acquire any record, reports, or other written statements regarding the Principal; (2) create, modify, or retain profession regarding documents needed on behalf of the Principal related to financial matters; (3) provide written responses to inquiries about Principal regarding financial matters.

_____ **M. Retirement Benefit Transactions.** The Principal authorizes the Agent to: (1) select a payment option under a retirement plan in which the Principal participates, including a plan for a self-employed individual; (2) make voluntary contributions to those plans; (3) exercise the investment powers available under a self-directed retirement plan; (4) make a rollover of benefits into another retirement plan; (5) if authorized by the plan, borrow from, sell assets to, purchase assets from, or request distributions from the plan; and (6) waive the right of the Principal to be a beneficiary of a joint or survivor annuity if the Principal is a spouse who is not employed.

_____ **N. Making Gifts To My Spouse, Children, More Remote Descendants, Parents, and Others.** The Principal authorizes the Agent to make gifts of any of the Principal's property to individuals or organizations within the limits of the annual exclusion under the Internal Revenue Code as the Agent determines to be in the Principal's best interest based on all relevant factors, including:(1) the value and nature of the Principal's property; (2) the Principal's foreseeable obligations and need for maintenance; 3) minimization of income, estate, inheritance, generation-skipping transfer or gift taxes; (4) eligibility for public benefits or assistance under a statute or governmental regulation; and (5) the Principal's personal history of making or joining in making gifts.

_____ **O. Tax Matters.** The Principal authorizes the Agent to: (1) prepare, sign, and file Federal, state, local, and foreign income, gift, payroll, Federal Insurance Contributions Act, and other tax returns, claims for refunds, requests for extension of time, petitions regarding tax matters, and any other tax-related documents, including receipts, offers, waivers, consents, including consents and agreements under the Internal Revenue Code, closing agreements, and any Power of Attorney required by the Internal Revenue Service or other taxing authority with respect to a tax year upon which the statute of limitations has not run; (2) pay taxes due, collect refunds, post bonds, receive confidential information, and contest deficiencies determined by the Internal Revenue Service or other taxing authority;

(3) exercise any election available to the Principal under Federal, state, local, or foreign tax law; and (4) act for the Principal in all tax matters for all periods before the Internal Revenue Service, and any other taxing authority.

_____   **P. Other Matters.** _____

_____

_____

_____

_____

_____

_____

_____

_____

_____   **Q. All Other Financial Matters.** Those matters not mentioned in this document are to be covered by this provision.

_____   **R. Full and Unqualified Authority to My Agent to Delegate Any or All of the Foregoing Powers To Any Person or Persons Whom My Agent May Select.**

_____   **S. Unlimited Power and Authority To Act In All Of The Above Situations (A Through R) Which I Have Initialed.** The Principal authorizes the Agent to: (1) demand, receive, and obtain by litigation or otherwise, money or other thing of value to which the Principal is, may become, or claims to be entitled, and conserve, invest, disburse, or use anything so received for the purposes intended; (2) contract in any manner with any person, on terms agreeable to the Agent, to accomplish a purpose of a transaction, and perform, rescind, reform, release, or modify the contract or another contract made by or on behalf of the Principal; (3) execute, acknowledge, seal, and deliver a deed, revocation, mortgage, security agreement, lease, notice, check, promissory note, electronic funds transfer, release, or other instrument or communication the Agent considers desirable to accomplish a purpose of a transaction, including creating a schedule of the Principal's property and attaching it to the Power of Attorney; (4) prosecute, defend, submit to arbitration or mediation, settle, and propose or accept a compromise with respect to, a claim existing in favor of or against the Principal or intervene in litigation relating to the claim; (5) seek on the Principal's behalf the assistance of a court to carry out an act authorized by the Principal in the Power of

Attorney; (6) engage, compensate, and discharge an attorney, accountant, expert witness, or other assistant; (7) keep appropriate records of each transaction, including an accounting of receipts and disbursements; (8) prepare, execute, and file a record, report, or other document the Agent considers desirable to safeguard or promote the Principal's interest under a statute or governmental regulation; (9) reimburse the Agent for expenditures properly made by the Agent in exercising the powers granted by the Power of Attorney; and (10) in general, do any other lawful act with respect to the power and all property related to the power.

I specifically DO NOT want the following person(s) to be involved in any manner in the decision-making regarding my financial matters: _____

_____.

To induce any third party to rely upon this Power of Attorney, I agree that any third party receiving a signed copy or facsimile of this document may rely upon such copy, and that revocation or termination of this Power of Attorney is ineffective as to such third party until actual notice or knowledge of such revocation or termination has been received by the third party.

My attorney-in-fact receives NO compensation for providing this service, or be liable to me, my estate, heirs, successors, or assigns for acting or refraining from acting under this document, except for willful misconduct or gross negligence.

I, _____, the Principal, sign my name to this

Power of Attorney this _____day of _____and, being first duly sworn, do declare to the undersigned authority that I sign and execute this instrument as my Power of Attorney and that I sign it willingly, or willingly direct another to sign for me, that I execute it as my free and voluntary act for the purposes expressed in the Power of Attorney and that I am eighteen years of age or older, of sound mind and under no constraint or undue influence, and that I have read and understand the contents of the notice at the beginning of this document.

Principal Signature: _____Date: _____

WITNESS STATEMENT

On this _____ day of _____ 20_____ we, _____

and _____, declare under penalty of perjury that the person who signed or acknowledged this document is personally known to me (or proved to me on the basis of convincing evidence) to be the Principal, that the Principal signed or acknowledged this durable Power of Attorney in my presence, that the Principal appears to be of sound mind and under no duress, fraud, or undue influence. We are not appointed as an Agent by this document. We are not related to the Principal by blood, marriage, or adoption. We would not be entitled to any portion of the Principal's estate on the Principal's death. We are not the attending physician of the Principal or an employee of the attending physician. We have no claim against any portion of the Principal's estate on the Principal's death. Furthermore, if we are an employee of a healthcare facility in which the Principal is a patient, we are not involved in providing direct patient care to the Principal and are not employed as an officer, director, partner, or business office employee of the healthcare facility or of any parent organization of the healthcare facility.

I sign my name to the foregoing Power of Attorney being first duly sworn and do declare to the undersigned authority that the Principal signs and executes this instrument as his/her Power of Attorney and that he\she signs it willingly, or willingly directs another to sign for him/her, and that I, in the presence and hearing of the Principal, sign this Power of Attorney as witness to the Principal's signing and that to the best of my knowledge the Principal is eighteen years of age or older, is of sound mind, and is under no constraint or undue influence.

_____   _____
Witness's Signature   Printed Name of Witness

_____
Address of Witness

_____   _____
Witness's Signature   Printed Name of Witness

_____
Address of Witness

_____   _____
Witness's Signature   Printed Name of Witness

_____
Address of Witness

NOTARY PUBLIC ACKNOWLEDGEMENT

The foregoing instrument was acknowledged, subscribed, and sworn to before me, this _____day

of _____, 20____, by _____, and witnessed

by _____, and _____,
personally known to me (or proved to me on the basis of satisfactory evidence) to be the person whose name is subscribed to the foregoing instrument, and acknowledged to me that he or she executed the same in his or her authorized capacity and that by his or her signature on the instrument, the person, or the entity upon behalf of which the person acted, executed the instrument.

Witness my hand and official seal.

_____

NOTARY PUBLIC for the State of _____

My Commission Expires: _____

[For Notary Seal or Stamp]

_____
NOTARY PUBLIC

POWER OF ATTORNEY ACKNOWLEDGEMENT AND ACCEPTANCE BY AGENT AND ALTERNATE AGENT

I, _____, have read the attached Power of Attorney, and I am the person identified as the Agent with the Financial Durable Power of Attorney for the Principal. I hereby acknowledge that I accept my appointment as Agent and attorney-in-fact, and, when I act as Agent, I will exercise the powers for the benefit of the Principal. I will keep the assets of the Principal separate from my assets, personal, professional, or otherwise. I will exercise reasonable caution and prudence, and I will keep a full and accurate record of all actions, receipts, and disbursements on behalf of the Principal.

Agent Signature: _____Date: _____

I, _____, have read the attached Power of Attorney, and I agree to act as an alternative Agent if the person identified as the Agent with the Financial Durable Power of Attorney for the Principal does not or cannot accept these duties. I accept my appointment as alternate Agent and attorney-in-fact, and if I am called upon to act as Agent, I will exercise the powers for the benefit of the Principal. I will keep the assets of the Principal separate from my assets, personal, professional, or otherwise. I will exercise reasonable caution and prudence, and I will keep a full and accurate record of all actions, receipts, and disbursements on behalf of the Principal.

Alternated Agent Signature: _____Date: _____

MINOR CHILD CARE LIMITED POWER OF ATTORNEY

I/We, _____,

whose address is _____

City of _____, in the County of _____,

in the State of _____, are the legal guardian(s) ("GUARDIAN") of the
following minor child(ren):

> Name: _____DOB: _____
>
> Name: _____DOB: _____
>
> Name: _____DOB: _____

(Collectively referred to as "CHILD") grant a limited and specific power of attorney to, and do

hereby appoint _____, whose address is

_____City _____,

County_____, State _____, "AGENT,"

and if Agent is unable or unwilling to make those decisions, I appoint as an alternate Agent

_____, whose address is _____

_____County_____

City_____in the State of _____.

Agent will act as attorney-in-fact and to have the full power and authority to perform only the
following acts that are **initialed below,** on Guardian's behalf, to the same extent Guardian could
do so personally if Guardian were personally present, with respect to the following matter to the
extent that Guardian is permitted by law to act through an agent. Consent given to:

_____   any necessary medical treatment for the Child, including any emergency medical
treatment, surgery, medication, hospitalization, any x-ray examination, anesthetic,
medical or surgical diagnosis or treatment, and hospital care which is deemed
advisable by, and is to be rendered under the general or specific supervision of
any physician and surgeon licensed under the provision of the Medical Practice
Act, whether such diagnosis or treatment is rendered at the office of said
physician or at a hospital, or any other necessary medical treatment; that may be

required. It is understood that this power is given in advance of any specific diagnosis, treatment, or hospital care being required, but is given to provide authority and power on the part of our Agent to give specific consent to any and all such diagnosis, treatment, or hospital care which the aforementioned physician in the exercise of his or her best judgment may deem advisable;

_____ enroll and withdraw the Child from any school or child care facility, and it is expressly the intent of Guardian that the Agent is given wide discretion in education matters and that all educational institutions recognize and follow the instructions of the Agent in regards to the education of the Child;

_____ exercise the same parental rights that Guardian may personally exercise regarding the care, custody and control of the Child, including providing discipline;

_____ authorize Agent to execute, acknowledge and deliver any instrument under seal or otherwise, and to do all things necessary to carry out the intent granted to Agent and authorize Agent to act fully and effectually as the Guardians may do if personally present, limited, however, to the purpose for which this limited power of attorney is executed.

_____ allow Agent to continue with the powers of attorney granted in this document even if any Guardian may become incapacitated or disabled, and Agent will only loose powers if Guardian revokes those powers which Guardian can do at any time either written or oral.

To induce any third party to rely on this Power of Attorney, any third party receiving a signed copy or facsimile of this document may rely on such copy, and that revocation or termination of this Power of Attorney is ineffective as to such third party until actual notice or knowledge of such revocation or termination has been received by the third party.

Agent receives NO compensation for providing this service, or will be liable to me, my estate, heirs, successors, or assigns for acting or refraining from acting under this document, except for willful misconduct or gross negligence.

I/We, _____,

the Guardian, sign to this Power of Attorney this _____ day of _____,

20_____ and, being first duly sworn, do declare to the undersigned authority sign and execute this instrument and sign willingly, or willingly direct another to sign for me, execute this Power of Attorney as a free and voluntary act for the purposes expressed in the Power of Attorney and am eighteen years of age or older, of sound mind and under no constraint or undue influence, and have read and understand the contents of the notice at the beginning of this document.

Guardian(s) Signature(s): _____

_____

Date: _____

WITNESS STATEMENT

On this _____ day of _____, 20_____, we, _____

and _____, declare under penalty of perjury that the person(s) who signed or acknowledged this document is personally known to me (or proved to me on the basis of convincing evidence) to be the Guardian, that the Guardian signed or acknowledged this durable Power of Attorney in my presence, that the Guardian appears to be of sound mind and under no duress, fraud, or undue influence. We are not appointed as an Agent by this document. We are not related to the Guardian by blood, marriage, or adoption.

I sign my name to the foregoing Power of Attorney being first duly sworn and do declare to the undersigned authority that the Guardian signs and executes this instrument as his/her Power of Attorney and that he\she signs it willingly, or willingly directs another to sign for him/her, and that I, in the presence and hearing of the Guardian, sign this Power of Attorney as witness to the Guardian's signing and that to the best of my knowledge the Guardian is eighteen years of age or older, of sound mind and under no constraint or undue influence.

_____   _____
Witness's Signature   Printed Name of Witness
_____
Address of Witness

_____   _____
Witness's Signature   Printed Name of Witness
_____
Address of Witness

NOTARY PUBLIC ACKNOWLEDGEMENT

The foregoing instrument was acknowledged, subscribed, and sworn to before me, this _____day

of _____, 20____, by _____, and witnessed

by _____, and _____,
personally known to me (or proved to me on the basis of satisfactory evidence) to be the person
whose name is subscribed to the foregoing instrument, and acknowledged to me that he or she
executed the same in his or her authorized capacity and that by his or her signature on the
instrument, the person, or the entity upon behalf of which the person acted, executed the
instrument.

Witness my hand and official seal.

_____

NOTARY PUBLIC for the State of _____

My Commission Expires: _____

[For Notary Seal or Stamp]

_____
NOTARY PUBLIC

MINOR CHILD CARE LIMITED POWER OF ATTORNEY ACKNOWLEDGEMENT AND ACCEPTANCE BY AGENT AND ALTERNATE AGENT

I, _____, have read the attached Power of Attorney, and I am the person identified as the Agent with the Minor Child Care Limited Power of Attorney. I hereby acknowledge that I accept my appointment as Agent and attorney-in-fact, and when I act as Agent I will exercise the powers for the benefit of the Guardian. I will exercise reasonable caution and prudence, and I will keep a full and accurate record of all actions, receipts, and disbursements on behalf of the Guardian.

Agent Signature: _____ Date: _____

I, _____, have read the attached Power of Attorney, and I agree to act as an alternative Agent if the person identified as the Agent with the Minor Child Care Limited Power of Attorney does not or cannot accept these duties. I accept my appointment as alternate Agent and attorney-in-fact, and if I am called on to act as Agent I will exercise the powers for the benefit of the Guardian and Child. I will exercise reasonable caution and prudence, and I will keep a full and accurate record of all actions, receipts, and disbursements on behalf of the Guardian.

Alternated Agent Signature: _____ Date: _____

POWER OF ATTORNEY REVOCATION

I/We, _____,

whose address is _____

City_____, County_____,

State_____, revoke the Power of Attorney dated_____

with the title _____and appointed Agent

_____whose address is_____

_____City _____,

County _____, State _____, and alternate Agent

_____, whose address is_____

_____, City_____,

County_____, State_____, in its entirety
without limitations, including revoking any appointment of any persons named in the above
Power of Attorney, the Agent, and the alternate Agent named in the document.

Revoking party's signature: _____Date: _____

NOTARY PUBLIC ACKNOWLEDGEMENT

The foregoing instrument was acknowledged, subscribed, and sworn to before me,

_____this ____day of _____,

20____, personally known to me (or proved to me on the basis of satisfactory evidence) to be the
person whose name is subscribed to the foregoing instrument, and acknowledged to me that he or
she executed the same in his or her authorized capacity and that by his or her signature on the
instrument, the person, or the entity upon behalf of which the person acted, executed the
instrument.
Witness my hand and official seal.
NOTARY PUBLIC for the State of _____, County of _____

My Commission Expires: _____

[For Notary Seal or Stamp]

_____
NOTARY PUBLIC

3. Trusts

Trusts Checklist

❑ If you are in the State of Florida or Florida is the State where this Living Trust will be legal, then you must also complete the Florida Witness Statement for Living Trusts (included in this book). No other State requires a witness to a Living Trust.

❑ Make additional copies of any specific pages you may need or tear them out of the book.

❑ Read over the blank form.

❑ If there are parts of the form you do not understand, read the applicable section within this book.

❑ Make adjustments to the form to meet your needs. If the paragraph or portion of the sample form does not apply, write "Does not apply" in the blank space.

❑ Complete the portions of the sample form with blank spaces. (Do NOT sign just yet.)

❑ Review the Living Trust you have completed to ensure that you have completed the entire form.

❑ Review the State Specific Information at PeerlessLegal.com.

❑ Meet with a Notary Public.

❑ Double-check the Living Trust for completeness and you understand its contents.

❑ Sign and date the Living Trust in the presence of the Notary Public.

❑ If your Living Trust is complicated, or includes numerous additions, then do not use this book or its contents for the sole purpose of creating a Living Trust. Contact a licensed attorney to help you create a Living Trust that meets your specific needs.

❑ Give a copy of the Living Trust to the named Successor Trustee and to the alternative Successor Trustee.

❑ Store a record of your final, signed Living Trust, in a safe place, along with all of your other important documents that you wish to pass on.

DECLARATION OF TRUST (Single Person)—LIVING TRUST OF _____

This DECLARATION OF TRUST ("DECLARATION") creates a trust known as The _____ _____Living Trust, and is entered into on this date _____("TRUST").

1. **ESTABLISHMENT OF TRUST.** This Declaration creates a Trust between _____ _____("GRANTOR"), and himself/herself as "TRUSTEE," whose address is _____ _____City _____, County _____, State _____.

   A. **CHOICE OF LAW.** The Trust will be governed by the laws of the State of _____, and all Trusts created by this Declaration, including Child's Trust, and actions taken by Trustee, are governed under this State's laws, subject to the Trustee's fiduciary duty to the Grantor and beneficiaries.

   B. **SEVERABILITY.** If any provision of this Declaration of Trust is ruled unenforceable, the remaining provisions will remain in effect.

   C. **AMENDMENTS.** This Trust includes any provisions added by amendments.

2. **TRUST PROPERTY.** Grantor has transferred, or will transfer, to the Trustee, the property that may be added to this Declaration in "**Schedule A**—Property Placed in Trust," including after-acquired property, that will be used for the benefit of the trust beneficiaries, and will be administered and distributed by the Trustee in accordance with this Declaration. Grantor is the legal and beneficial owner of all property in this Declaration and all property that may be added.

3. **POWERS OF THE GRANTOR.** The Grantor has the powers deemed necessary and appropriate to administer this Trust, including powers granted by the State where this Declaration is governed and is subject to the fiduciary duties to the Grantor and beneficiaries. The powers of this Declaration include, but are not limited to, the powers to:

A. AMEND OR REVOKE DECLARATION.

1) BY GRANTOR. The Grantor reserves the power to amend or revoke this Declaration at any time during Grantor's lifetime, without notifying any beneficiary.

2) BY OTHERS. The right to amend or revoke this Declaration is personal to the Grantor, and any conservator, guardian, or other party may NOT exercise Grantor's power to amend or revoke this Declaration without the Grantor specifically granting the power in a separate Durable Power of Attorney.

B. RETAIN ALL RIGHTS TO TRUST PROPERTY.
All rights to any income, profits, and control of the Trust property are retained by the Grantor until the death of the Grantor.

C. HOMESTEAD.
If the Grantor's principal residence is held in this Trust, Grantor has the right to possess and occupy the residence for Grantor's entire life, rent-free and without charge, except for taxes, insurance, maintenance, and related costs and expenses. This right is intended to give Grantor a beneficial interest in the property and to ensure that Grantor does not lose eligibility for any State homestead tax exemption for which Grantor otherwise qualifies.

D. INCAPACITY OF GRANTOR.
If Grantor becomes incapacitated, physically or mentally, to where Grantor cannot manage this Trust then, whether or not a court has declared the Grantor incompetent or in need of conservator or guardian, the person(s) named as Successor Trustee will serve as Trustee (as defined in Section 4.B.). The determination of the Grantor's capacity to manage this Trust will be made by the Successor Trustee (as defined in Section 4.B.) who is reasonably available to make such a determination in a timely manner. If there are multiple successor trustees, and a majority of the Successor Trustees (as defined in Section 4.B.) state, in writing, that, in their opinion, Grantor is no longer reasonably capable of serving as trustee, the Successor Trustee (as defined in Section 4.B.) will serve as Trustee. The Successor Trustee (as defined in Section 4.B.) will pay

trust income, at least annually, to, or for the benefit of, the Grantor and may spend any amount of Trust principal necessary for the needs of the Grantor, until the Grantor is no longer incapacitated or until the Grantor's death.

E. **DEATH OF GRANTOR.** At Grantor's death, this Trust will become irrevocable. This Trust cannot be altered or amended, except as provided in this Declaration, and it may NOT be terminated except through distributions permitted by this Declaration. Trustee must pay out Trust property necessary for payment of the Grantor's debts, estate taxes, and expenses of the Grantor's illnesses and cost of final arrangements, such as burial plot or cremation costs. All of the property in the Trust must be distributed outright to the Beneficiaries (as provided in Section 5.A.) subject to any provisions in this Declaration that creates child's trusts or creates custodianships under the Uniform Transfers to Minors Act.

4. **TRUSTEES.**

A. **TRUSTEE.** The Trustee is identified in Section 1. Establishment of Trust.

B. **SUCCESSOR TRUSTEE.** Upon the death or incapacity (as defined in Section 3.D. and Section 3.E.) of the Trustee, _____
will serve as the "SUCCESSOR TRUSTEE." The Successor Trustee will become the Trustee at that time. If the Successor Trustee is not able to serve or continue to serve as successor trustee, then the alternate Successor Trustee will be _____
_____.

_____ The Successor Trustee will have the complete and independent authority to act for, and represent the Trust.

[OR] (Select only one by placing your initials next to the clause.)

_____ The Successor Trustee must obtain consent, in writing, from all of the beneficiaries whose Trust property is affected by a transaction.

C. **TRUSTEE'S RESPONSIBILITY.** The Trustee will serve as Trustee of all of the Trusts created in this Declaration, including any Child's Trust.

D. TRUSTEE RESIGNATION. Any Trustee may resign at any time by signing a notice of resignation and must deliver the notice of registration to the alternate Trustee under Section 4.B.

E. POWERS AND DUTIES.

    1)   POWERS TO APPOINT SUCCESSOR TRUSTEE. If the entire successor Trustees named in this Declaration, Section 4.B. cease to, or are unable to, serve as Trustee, any Trustee may appoint an additional Trustee or Successor Trustee to serve in the order nominated. The appointment must be made in writing, signed by the Trustee, and notarized.

    2)   SPECIFIC DUTIES. The Trustee's powers include, but are not limited to, the power to:

1. sell Trust property, and borrow money and to encumber Trust property, including mortgage, deed by trust, or otherwise, any Trust real estate.

2. manage Trust real estate as if the Trustee were the absolute owner, including the power to lease (even lease terms that extend beyond the period of the Trust), grant options to lease Trust real estate, make repairs or alterations, and to insure against loss.

3. sell or grant options for the sale or exchange of any Trust property, including stocks, bonds, debentures, and any other form of security or security account, at public or private sale for cash or credit.

4. invest Trust property in property of any kind, including, but not limited to, bonds, debentures, notes, mortgages, stocks, stock options, stock futures, and buying on margin.

5. receive additional property from any source and add to any Trust created by this Declaration.

6. employ and pay reasonable fees to accountants, lawyers, or

investment experts for information or advice relating to the Trust.

7. deposit and hold Trust funds in both interest-bearing and non-interest-bearing accounts.

8. deposit funds in bank or other accounts insured or uninsured by the FDIC.

9. enter into electronic fund transfer or safe deposit arrangements with financial institutions.

10. continue any business of the Grantor.

11. institute or defend legal actions concerning the Trust or Grantor's affairs.

12. execute any document necessary to administer any Child's Trust created in this Declaration.

13. diversify investments, including authority to decide that some or all of the Trust property need not produce income.

3)   **PAYMENT OF DEBTS AND TA.** The Grantor's debts and death taxes are to be paid by the Trustee from the following Trust property: _____

_____.

If the property is not sufficient to pay all the Grantor's debts and death taxes, then the Trustee must make a determination as to how such debts and death taxes will be paid from Trust property.

4)   **ACCOUNTING.** No accountings or similar reports are required by Trustee.

F. **NO TRUSTEE BOND REQUIRED.** No bond is required of any Trustee.

G. **NO TRUSTEE COMPENSATION.** No Trustee is to receive any compensation in any form for serving as Trustee, except that a Trustee may be entitled to reasonable compensation, as determined by the Trustee, for serving as a Trustee of a Child's Trust created by this Declaration, or for serving as Trustee if the Grantor is incapacitated.

H. TRUSTEE LIABILITY. With respect to the exercise or non-exercise of discretionary powers granted by this Declaration, the Trustee is not liable for actions taken in good faith.

5. **BENEFICIARIES.** On Grantor's death, the property listed on **Schedule A** is to be distributed to the beneficiaries named in this Section.

    A. PRIMARY AND ALTERNATE BENEFICIARIES.

        1)   The property identified as _____

_____

_____

is left in Trust to _____

(the "PRIMARY BENEFICIARY"). If the primary beneficiary does not survive Grantor, or rejects the property, then to _____

_____

(the "ALTERNATE PRIMARY BENEFICIARY").

        2)   The property identified as _____

_____

_____

is left in Trust to _____

(the "PRIMARY BENEFICIARY"). If the primary beneficiary does not survive Grantor, or rejects the property, then to _____

_____

(the "ALTERNATE PRIMARY BENEFICIARY").

        3)   The property identified as _____

_____

_____

is left in Trust to _____

(the "PRIMARY BENEFICIARY"). If the primary beneficiary does not survive Grantor, or rejects the property, then to _____

_____

(the "ALTERNATE PRIMARY BENEFICIARY").

B. **RESIDUARY BENEFICIARY.** The remainder of the property in **Schedule A** that is not assigned and validly disposed of in Section 5.A. or 6.F. will go to _____

_____

("RESIDUARY BENEFICIARY") and if the Residuary Beneficiary does not take the property then _____

will take the property as the "ALTERNATE RESIDUARY BENEFICIARY."

6. **CHILD(REN)'S SUBTRUST(S).** All Trust property left to any of the minor or young adult beneficiaries listed below in Section 6.A. will be retained in Trust for each named child beneficiary in a separate Trust that can be identified and referred to by adding the name of that Trust's beneficiary to the name of this Trust. The following terms apply to each Child's Trust:

A. **TRUST BENEFICIARIES AND AGE LIMITS.** A Child's Trust ends when the beneficiary of that Trust becomes 35, except as otherwise specified in this Section:

Trust for   Ends at Age

_____   _____

_____   _____

_____   _____

_____   _____

_____   _____

B. **TRUSTEE POWERS AND DUTIES.**

1)   Until a Child's Trust ends, the Trustee may distribute or use assets for the benefit of the beneficiary as the Trustee deems necessary for the beneficiary's health, support, maintenance, or education. Education includes, but is not limited to, college, graduate, professional, and vocational studies, and reasonably related living expenses.

2) In deciding whether to make a distribution to the beneficiary, the Trustee may take into account the beneficiary's other income, resources, and sources of support.

3) Any Child's Trust income that is not distributed to a beneficiary by the Trustee will accumulate and add to the principal of the Trust for that beneficiary.

4) The Trustee of a Child's Trust is not required to make any accounting or report to the Trust beneficiary.

C. NO ASSIGNMENT OF BENEFICIARY INTEREST. The interests of the beneficiary of a Child's Trust cannot be transferred by voluntary or involuntary assignment or by operation of law before actual receipt by the beneficiary. These interests are free from the claims of creditors and from attachments, execution, bankruptcy, or other legal process to the fullest extent permitted by law.

D. TRUSTEE COMPENSATION. Any Trustee of a Child's Trust created under this Declaration will be entitled to reasonable compensation out of the Trust assets for ordinary and extraordinary services, and for all services in connection with the termination of any Trust.

E. TERMINATION. A Child's Trust will end when any of the following events occur:

1) the beneficiary reaches the age specified in Section 6.A. If the Trust ends for this reason, the remaining principal and accumulated income of the Trust will be given outright to the beneficiary.

2) the beneficiary dies. If the Trust ends for this reason, the Trust property will pass to the beneficiary's heirs.

3) the Trustee distributes all Trust property under the provisions of this Declaration.

F. CUSTODIANSHIPS UNDER THE UNIFORM TRANSFERS TO MINORS ACT.

1)   All property that the minor beneficiary, _____,
is entitled to under this Trust is given to _____
to act as custodian for the beneficiary under the State of _____
Uniform Transfers to Minors Act, until the beneficiary reaches the age
_____.

2)   All property that the minor beneficiary, _____,
is entitled to under this Trust is given to _____
to act as custodian for the beneficiary under the State of _____
Uniform Transfers to Minors Act, until the beneficiary reaches the age
_____.

3)   All property that the minor beneficiary, _____,
is entitled to under this Trust is given to _____
to act as custodian for the beneficiary under the State of _____
Uniform Transfers to Minors Act, until the beneficiary reaches the age
_____.

4)   All property that the minor beneficiary, _____,
is entitled to under this Trust is given to _____
to act as custodian for the beneficiary under the State of _____
Uniform Transfers to Minors Act, until the beneficiary reaches the age
_____.

CERTIFICATION BY GRANTOR. I certify that I have read this Declaration and that it correctly states the terms and conditions under which the Trust property is to be held, managed, and disposed of by the Trustee, and I approve the Declaration.

_____   _____

Grantor and Trustee   Date

NOTARY PUBLIC ACKNOWLEDGEMENT

The foregoing instrument was acknowledged, subscribed, and sworn to before me,

_____ this _____ day of _____, 20_____, personally known to me (or proved to me on the basis of satisfactory evidence) to be the person whose name is subscribed to the foregoing instrument, and acknowledged to me that he or she executed the same in his or her authorized capacity and that by his or her signature on the instrument, the person, or the entity upon behalf of which the person acted, executed the instrument.

Witness my hand and official seal.

_____

NOTARY PUBLIC for the State of _____

My Commission Expires: _____

[For Notary Seal or Stamp]

_____
NOTARY PUBLIC

Schedule A—Property Placed in Trust

All the grantor's interest in the following property: _____

_____

_____

_____

_____

_____

_____

_____

_____

_____

_____

_____

_____

_____

_____

_____

_____

_____

_____

_____

_____

_____

DECLARATION OF TRUST (Married)—LIVING TRUST

OF_____AND _____

This DECLARATION OF TRUST ("DECLARATION") creates a trust known as "The _____and _____Living Trust", and is entered into on this _____day of _____, 20____ ("TRUST").

1. **ESTABLISHMENT OF TRUST.** This Declaration creates a Trust between _____ _____whose address is _____ _____City _____, County _____, State _____ ("WIFE"), and _____ whose address is _____ City _____, County _____, State _____ ("HUSBAND"), and collectively the Wife and Husband are the "GRANTORS" or "TRUSTEES".

   A. **CHOICE OF LAW.** The Trust will be governed by the laws of the State of _____, and all Trusts created by this Declaration, including Child's Trust, and actions taken by Trustee are governed under this State's laws, subject to the Trustee's fiduciary duty to the Grantors and beneficiaries.

   B. **SEVERABILITY.** If any provision of this Declaration of Trust is ruled unenforceable, the remaining provisions shall nevertheless remain in effect.

   C. **AMENDMENTS.** This Trust includes any provisions added by amendments.

2. **TRUST PROPERTY.** Grantors have transferred, or will transfer, to the Trustees, the property that may be added by either Grantors to any Trust in this Declaration including "**Schedule A**—Shared Property Placed in Trust," **Schedule B**—Wife's Separate Property Place in Trust" and "**Schedule C**—Husband's Separate Property Place in Trust."

   A. **AFTER-ACQUIRED PROPERTY.** Adding after-acquired property by either Grantor to any part of this Declaration is also permitted and will be used for the benefit of the Trust beneficiaries and will be administered and distributed by the Trustees in accordance with this Declaration.

B. **ORIGINAL CHARACTER RETAINED.** Until the death of either Grantor, property transferred to any part of this Trust will retain its original character as detailed in Section 3.B. If the Trust is revoked, the Trustee must distribute the Trust property to the Grantors based on the same ownership rights they had before the property was transferred to the Trust.

C. **LEGEL AND BENEFICIAL OWNERS OF PROPERTY.** Grantors are the legal and beneficial owner of all property in this Declaration and all property that may be added.

D. **TRUST PROPERTY ADMINISTRATION.**

    1) **TERMINOLOGY.** The first Grantor to die will be called the "DECEASED SPOUSE," and the living Grantor shall be called the "SURVIVING SPOUSE."

    2) **DEATH OF SPOUSE TRUST PROPERTY DIVISION DISTRIBUTION.**

        1. On the death of the Deceased Spouse, the Trustee will divide the Trust property listed on **Schedules A**, **B**, and **C** into two separate trusts, Trust 1 and Trust 2 according to Sections 2.D.2.2 and 2.D.2.3. The Trustee shall serve as Trustee of Trust 1 and Trust 2 (as defined in Sections 2.D.2.2 and 2.D.2.3.).

        2. "TRUST 1" will contain all the property in the Trust owned by the Deceased Spouse at the time it was transferred to the Trustee, plus shared ownership property with a total value equal to one-half of the total value at the time of the Deceased Spouse's death of shared ownership property, plus accumulated income, appreciation in value, and the like, attributable to the ownership interest of the Deceased Spouse, and his or her share of all property acquired in the Trust's or Trustees' names. Trust 1 becomes irrevocable at the death of the Deceased Spouse. The Trustee must distribute the property in Trust 1 to the beneficiaries named by the Deceased

Spouse in Section 5, subject to any provision of this Declaration that creates a Child's Trusts or creates custodianships under the Uniform Transfers to Minors Act.

3. "TRUST 2" will contain all the property in the Trust owned by the Surviving Spouse at the time it was transferred to the Trust, plus accumulated income, appreciation in value, and the like attributable to the ownership interest of the Surviving Spouse and any Trust property left by the Deceased Spouse to the Surviving Spouse.

   a. Until the death of the Surviving Spouse, all rights to all income, profits, and control of property in Trust 2 will be retained by, or distributed to, the Surviving Spouse.

   b. The Surviving Spouse can amend or revoke Trust 2 at any time during their lifetime, without notifying any beneficiary.

   c. On Surviving Spouse's death, Trust 2 will become irrevocable, and the property in Trust 2 will be distributed to the beneficiaries listed in Section 5, subject to any provision of this Declaration that creates a Child's Trusts or creates custodianships under the Uniform Transfers to Minors Act.

4. The Trustee will have exclusive authority to determine the paperwork and record keeping necessary to establish Trust 1 and Trust 2.

5. Any Trust property left by the Deceased Spouse to the Surviving Spouse will remain in the Surviving Spouse's revocable Trust, Trust 2, without necessity of a formal transfer to that Trust.

3. **POWERS OF THE GRANTORS.** The Grantors have the powers deemed necessary and appropriate to administer this Trust, including powers granted by the State where this

Declaration is governed and is subject to the fiduciary duties to the Grantors and beneficiaries. The powers of this Declaration include, but are not limited to, the powers to:

A. AMEND OR REVOKE DECLARATION.

1) **BY GRANTORSS.** Either Grantor reserves the power to amend or revoke this Declaration at any time during Grantor's lifetime, without notifying any beneficiary, but must provide written notice to the other Grantor prior to making the amendment or revocation.

2) **BY OTHERS.** The right to amend or revoke this Declaration is personal to the Grantors, and a conservator, guardian, or anyone else may NOT exercise Grantors' power to amend or revoke this Declaration without the Grantors specifically granting the power in a separate Durable Power of Attorney.

B. RETAIN ALL RIGHTS TO TRUST PROPERTY.

1) **SCHEDULE A.** All rights to any income, profits, and control of the Trust property in **Schedule A** are retained by both of the Grantors until the death of both Grantors, and are shared property.

2) **SCHEDULE B.** All rights to any income, profits, and control of the Trust property in **Schedule B** are retained by the Wife, until the death of the Wife, and retain its character as being separate property of the Wife.

3) **SCHEDULE C.** All rights to any income, profits, and control of the Trust property in **Schedule C** are retained by the Husband, until the death of the Husband, and retain its character as being separate property of the Husband.

C. HOMESTEAD.
If the Grantors' principle residence is held in this Trust, Grantors have the right to possess and occupy the residence for Grantors' entire life, rent-free and without charge, except for taxes, insurance, maintenance, and related costs and expenses. This right is intended to give Grantors a beneficial interest in the property and to ensure that Grantors do not lose eligibility for any

State homestead tax exemption for which either Grantor may otherwise qualify.

D. **DEATH OR INCAPACITY OF EITHER GRANTOR.** If either Grantor dies or becomes incapacitated, physically or mentally, to where Grantor cannot manage this Trust, and whether or not a court has declared the Grantor incompetent or in need of conservator or guardian, the other spouse will serve as sole Trustee of all Trust, including any Child's Trust created under this Declaration.

E. **INCAPACITY OF BOTH GRANTORS.** The Successor Trustee must pay Trust income at least annually to, or for the benefit of, the Grantors and may also spend any amount of Trust income or Trust principal necessary, in the Successor Trustee's discretion, for the needs of the Grantors, until the Grantors, or either of them, are again able to manage their own affairs, or until their deaths. The determination of the Grantors' capacity to manage this Trust will be made by

_____,

who are reasonably available when the successor Trustee (or any of them, if two or more are named to serve together) requests their opinion. If a majority of these persons state, in writing, that in their opinion the Grantors are no longer reasonably capable of serving as Trustee, the successor Trustee will serve as Trustee.

F. **SIMULTANEOUS DEATH OF THE GRANTORS.** If both Grantors die simultaneously, or under such circumstances as to make it difficult or impossible to determine who predeceased the other, it will conclusively be presumed that both died at the same moment, and neither Grantor will be presumed to have survived the other, and the Trusts in this Declaration will become irrevocable. The Trustee will distribute the Trust property to the named beneficiaries.

4. **TRUSTEES.**

A. **TRUSTEES.** The Trustees are identified in Section 1. Establishment of Trust. Either Grantor may act as Trustee of any of the Trusts in this Declaration. The singular "Trustee" also includes the plural.

B. SUCCESSOR TRUSTEES. Upon the death or incapacity (as defined in Section 3.D. and Section 3.E.) of the surviving spouse, the "SUCCESSOR TRUSTEES" will be _____, and the Successor Trustees will become the Trustees at that time. If the Successor Trustees are not able to serve or continue serve as successor trustee, then the alternate Successor Trustees will be _____.
Successor Trustees:

> _____ will have the complete and independent authority to act for and represent the Trust.

> **[OR]** [select only one]

> _____ must all consent, in writing, to any transaction involving the Trust or Trust property.

C. TRUSTEES' RESPONSIBILITY. The Trustees will serve as Trustees of all of the Trusts created in this Declaration, including any Child's Trust.

D. TRUSTEES RESIGNATION. Any Trustees may resign at any time by signing a notice of resignation and must deliver the notice of registration to the alternate Trustees under Section 4.B.

E. POWERS AND DUTIES.

> **1)** **POWERS TO APPOINT SUCCESSOR TRUSTEES.** If the entire successor Trustees named in this Declaration, Section 4.B. cease to, or are unable to, serve as Trustees, any of the Trustees may appoint an additional Trustee or Successor Trustee to serve in the order nominated. The appointment must be made in writing, signed by the Trustees, and notarized.

> **2)** **SPECIFIC DUTIES.** The Trustees' powers include, but are not limited to, the power to:

>> 1. sell Trust property, and borrow money and to encumber Trust property, including mortgage, deed by trust, or otherwise any Trust

real estate.

2. manage Trust real estate as if the Trustees were the absolute owner, including the power to lease (even lease terms that extend beyond the period of the Trust), grant options to lease Trust real estate, make repairs or alterations, and to insure against loss.

3. sell or grant options for the sale or exchange of any Trust property, including stocks, bonds, debentures, and any other form of security or security account, at public or private sale for cash or credit.

4. invest Trust property in property of any kind, including, but not limited to, bonds, debentures, notes, mortgages, stocks, stock options, stock futures, and buying on margin.

5. receive additional property from any source and add to any Trust created by this Declaration.

6. employ and pay reasonable fees to accountants, lawyers, or investment experts for information or advice relating to the Trust.

7. deposit and hold Trust funds in both interest-bearing and non-interest-bearing accounts.

8. deposit funds in bank or other accounts insured or uninsured by the FDIC.

9. enter into electronic fund transfer or safe deposit arrangements with financial institutions.

10. continue any business of the Grantors.

11. institute or defend legal actions concerning the Trust or Grantors' affairs.

12. execute any document necessary to administer any Child's Trust created in this Declaration.

13. diversify investments, including authority to decide that some or

all of the Trust property need not produce income.

3) **PAYMENT OF DEBTS AND TAXES.**

1. **WIFE.** The Wife's debts and death taxes are to be paid by the Trustees from the following Trust property: _____ _____.

If the property is not sufficient to pay all of the Wife's debts and death taxes, then the Trustees must make a determination as to how such debts and death taxes will be paid from other Trust property.

2. **HUSBAND.** The Husband's debts and death taxes are to be paid by the Trustees from the following Trust property:_____ _____. If the property is not sufficient to pay all of the Husband's debts and death taxes, then the Trustees must make a determination as to how such debts and death taxes will be paid from other Trust property.

4) **ACCOUNTING.** No accountings or similar reports are required by Trustees.

F. **NO TRUSTEES BOND REQUIRED.** No bond is required of any Trustees.

G. **NO TRUSTEES COMPENSATION.** No Trustees are to receive any compensation in any form for serving as Trustees, except that Trustees may be entitled to reasonable compensation, as determined by the Trustees, for serving as Trustees of a Child's Trust created by this Declaration, or for serving as Trustees if the Grantors are incapacitated.

H. **TRUSTEE LIABILITY.** With respect to the exercise or non-exercise of discretionary powers granted by this Declaration, the Trustee is not liable for actions taken in good faith.

5. **BENEFICIARIES.**

A. **WIFE'S PRIMARY AND ALTERNATE BENEFICIARIES.** On the Wife's death, Trust property owned by Wife, as her share of the Trust property listed on

Schedule A and any separate property listed on **Schedule B** are to be distributed as specified to the beneficiaries named in this Section.

    1)   **WIFE'S SPECIFIC BENEFICIARIES.**

    1. The property identified as _____

_____

_____

is left in Trust to_____

_____, the primary beneficiary.

If the primary beneficiary does not survive Grantors or rejects the

property, then to _____,

the alternate beneficiary.

    2. The property identified as _____

_____

_____

is left in Trust to_____

_____, the primary beneficiary.

If the primary beneficiary does not survive Grantors or rejects the

property, then to _____,

the alternate beneficiary.

    3. The property identified as _____

_____

_____

is left in Trust to_____

_____, the primary beneficiary.

If the primary beneficiary does not survive Grantors or rejects the

property, then to _____,

the alternate beneficiary.

B. WIFE'S RESIDUARY BENEFICIARY. The remainder of the property in **Schedule A** that is not assigned and validly disposed of in Section 6.A. will go to

("WIFE'S RESIDUARY BENEFICIARY") and if the Wife's Residuary Beneficiary does not take the property then to _____ _____will take the property as alternate Wife's Residuary Beneficiary.

C. HUSBAND'S PRIMARY AND ALTERNATE BENEFICIARIES. On the Husband's death, Trust property owned by Husband, as his share of the Trust property listed on **Schedule A** and any separate property listed on **Schedule C** are to be distributed as specified to the beneficiaries named in this Section.

    1)   **HUSBAND'S SPECIFIC BENEFICIARIES.**

        1. The property identified as _____

_____

_____

is left in Trust to_____

_____, the primary beneficiary. If the primary beneficiary does not survive Grantors or rejects the property, then to _____, the alternate beneficiary.

        2. The property identified as _____

_____

_____

is left in Trust to_____

_____, the primary beneficiary. If the primary beneficiary does not survive Grantors or rejects the property, then to _____, the alternate beneficiary.

        3. The property identified as _____

_____

_____

is left in Trust to_____

_____, the primary beneficiary.

If the primary beneficiary does not survive Grantors or rejects the

property, then to _____,

the alternate beneficiary.

D. HUSBAND'S RESIDUARY BENEFICIARY. The remainder of the property in

Schedule A that is not assigned and validly disposed of in Section 6.A. will go to

_____

("HUSBAND'S RESIDUARY BENEFICIARY") and if the Husband's Residuary

Beneficiary does not take the property then to _____

_____will take the property as alternate Husband's

Residuary Beneficiary.

6. **CHILD(REN)'S SUBTRUST(S).** All Trust property left to any of the minor or young

adult beneficiaries listed below in Section 6.A. will be retained in Trust for each named

child beneficiary in a separate Trust that can be identified and referred to by adding the

name of that Trust's beneficiary to the name of this Trust. The following terms apply to

each Child's Trust:

A. TRUST BENEFICIARIES AND AGE LIMITS. A Child's Trust ends when the

beneficiary of that Trust reaches the age of 35, except as otherwise specified in

this Section:

Trust for   Ends at Age

_____   _____

_____   _____

_____   _____

_____   _____

B. TRUSTEES POWERS AND DUTIES.

1) Until a Child's Trust ends, the Trustees may distribute or use assets for the benefit of the beneficiary as the Trustees deems necessary for the beneficiary's health, support, maintenance, or education. Education includes, but is not limited to, college, graduate, professional, and vocational studies, and reasonably related living expenses.

2) In deciding whether to make a distribution to the beneficiary, the Trustees may take into account the beneficiary's other income, resources, and sources of support.

3) Any Child's Trust income that is not distributed to a beneficiary by the Trustees will accumulate and add to the principal of the Trust for that beneficiary.

4) The Trustees of a Child's Trust are not required to make any accounting or report to the Trust beneficiary.

C. NO ASSIGNMENT OF BENEFICIARY INTEREST.
The interests of the beneficiary of a Child's Trust cannot be transferred by voluntary or involuntary assignment or by operation of law before actual receipt by the beneficiary. These interests are free from the claims of creditors and from attachments, execution, bankruptcy, or other legal process to the fullest extent permitted by law.

D. TRUSTEES COMPENSATION.
Any Trustees of a Child's Trust created under this Declaration will be entitled to reasonable compensation out of the Trust assets for ordinary and extraordinary services, and for all services in connection with the termination of any Trust.

E. TERMINATION.
A Child's Trust will end when any of the following events occur:

1) the beneficiary reaches the age specified in Section 6.A. If the Trust ends for this reason, the remaining principal and accumulated income of the Trust will be given outright to the beneficiary.

2)   the beneficiary dies. If the Trust ends for this reason, the Trust property will pass to the beneficiary's heirs.

3)   the Trustees distributes all Trust property under the provisions of this Declaration.

F. CUSTODIANSHIPS UNDER THE UNIFORM TRANSFERS TO MINORS ACT.

1)   All property that the minor beneficiary, _____, is entitled to under this Trust is given to _____ to act as custodian for the beneficiary under the State of _____ Uniform Transfers to Minors Act, until the beneficiary reaches the age _____.

2)   All property that the minor beneficiary, _____, is entitled to under this Trust is given to _____ to act as custodian for the beneficiary under the State of _____ Uniform Transfers to Minors Act, until the beneficiary reaches the age _____.

3)   All property that the minor beneficiary, _____, is entitled to under this Trust is given to _____ to act as custodian for the beneficiary under the State of _____ Uniform Transfers to Minors Act, until the beneficiary reaches the age _____.

4)   All property that the minor beneficiary, _____, is entitled to under this Trust is given to _____ to act as custodian for the beneficiary under the State of _____ Uniform Transfers to Minors Act, until the beneficiary reaches the age _____.

7. **CERTIFICATION BY GRANTORS.** I certify that I have read this Declaration and that it correctly states the terms and conditions under which the Trust property is to be held, managed, and disposed of by the Trustees, and I approve the Declaration.

_____   _____

Grantors and Trustees, Wife   Date

_____   _____

Grantors and Trustees, Husband   Date

NOTARY PUBLIC ACKNOWLEDGEMENT

The foregoing instrument was acknowledged, subscribed, and sworn to before me,

_____this _____day of _____, 20_____, personally known to me (or proved to me on the basis of satisfactory evidence) to be the person whose name is subscribed to the foregoing instrument, and acknowledged to me that he or she executed the same in his or her authorized capacity and that by his or her signature on the instrument, the person, or the entity upon behalf of which the person acted, executed the instrument.

Witness my hand and official seal.

_____

NOTARY PUBLIC for the State of _____

My Commission Expires: _____

[For Notary Seal or Stamp]

_____
NOTARY PUBLIC

Schedule A—Shared Property Placed in Trust

All the grantor's interest in the following property: _____

_____

_____

_____

_____

_____

_____

_____

_____

_____

_____

_____

_____

_____

_____

_____

_____

_____

_____

_____

Schedule B—Wife's Separate Property Placed in Trust

All of Wife's interest in the following property: _____

_____

_____

_____

_____

_____

_____

_____

_____

_____

_____

_____

_____

_____

_____

_____

_____

_____

_____

_____

_____

_____

Schedule C—Husband's Separate Property Placed in Trust

All of Husband's interest in the following property: _____

_____

_____

_____

_____

_____

_____

_____

_____

_____

_____

_____

_____

_____

_____

_____

_____

_____

_____

_____

_____

DECLARATION OF TRUST (Married)—AB LIVING TRUST

OF_____AND_____

This DECLARATION OF TRUST ("DECLARATION") creates a trust known as The _____and _____Living Trust, and is entered into on this _____ day of _____, 20____("TRUST").

1. **ESTABLISHMENT OF TRUST.** This Declaration creates a Trust between _____ _____whose address is _____ _____City _____, County _____, State _____ ("WIFE"), and _____ whose address is _____ City _____, County _____, State _____("HUSBAND"), and collectively the Wife and Husband are the "GRANTORS" or "TRUSTEES".

   A. **CHOICE OF LAW.** The Trust will be governed by the laws of the State of _____, and all Trusts created by this Declaration, including Trust A, Trust B, Child's Trust, and actions taken by Trustee are governed under this State's laws, subject to the Trustee's fiduciary duty to the Grantors and beneficiaries.

   B. **SEVERABILITY.** If any provision of this Declaration of Trust is ruled unenforceable, the remaining provisions shall nevertheless remain in effect.

   C. **AMENDMENTS.** This Trust includes any provisions added by amendments.

2. **TRUST PROPERTY.** Grantors have transferred, or will transfer, to the Trustees the property that may be added by either Grantors to any Trust in this Declaration including "**Schedule A—Shared Property Placed in Trust,**" **Schedule B**—Wife's Separate Property Place in Trust" and "**Schedule C**—Husband's Separate Property Place in Trust."

   A. **AFTER-ACQUIRED PROPERTY.** Adding after-acquired property by either Grantor to any part of this Declaration is also permitted and will be used for the benefit of the Trust beneficiaries and will be administered and distributed by the

Trustees in accordance with this Declaration.

B. ORIGINAL CHARACTER RETAINED. Until the death of either Grantor, property transferred to any part of this Trust will retain its original character as detailed in Section 3.B. If the Trust is revoked, the Trustee must distribute the Trust property to the Grantors based on the same ownership rights they had before the property was transferred to the Trust.

C. LEGEL AND BENEFICIAL OWNERS OF PROPERTY. Grantors are the legal and beneficial owner of all property in this Declaration and all property that may be added.

3. **POWERS OF THE GRANTORS.** The Grantors have the powers deemed necessary and appropriate to administer this Trust, including powers granted by the State where this Declaration is governed and is subject to the fiduciary duties to the Grantors and beneficiaries. The powers of this Declaration include, but are not limited to, the powers to:

   A. AMEND OR REVOKE DECLARATION.

   1) **BY GRANTORS.** Either Grantor reserves the power to amend or revoke this Trust at any time during Grantors' lifetime, without notifying any beneficiary, but must provide writing to the other Grantor prior to making the amendment or revocation, except as provided elsewhere in this Declaration. After the death of a spouse, the surviving spouse can amend their revocable living trust, Trust B, The Surviving Spouse's Trust, as defined in Section 6.A.3. and 6.B.3, and in Section 7.

   2) **BY OTHERS.** The right to amend or revoke this Declaration is personal to the Grantors, and a conservator, guardian, or anyone else cannot exercise Grantors' power to amend or revoke this Declaration without the Grantors specifically granting the power in a separate Durable Power of Attorney.

   B. RETAIN ALL RIGHTS TO TRUST PROPERTY.

1) **SCHEDULE A.** All rights to any income, profits, and control of the Trust property in **Schedule A** are retained by both of the Grantors until the death of both Grantors, and are shared property.

2) **SCHEDULE B.** All rights to any income, profits, and control of the Trust property in **Schedule B** are retained by the Wife until the death of the Wife, and retain its character as being separate property of the Wife.

3) **SCHEDULE C.** All rights to any income, profits, and control of the Trust property in **Schedule C** are retained by the Husband until the death of the Husband, and retain its character as being separate property of the Husband.

C. **HOMESTEAD.** If the Grantors' principal residence is held in this Trust, Grantors have the right to possess and occupy the residence for Grantors' entire life, rent-free and without charge, except for taxes, insurance, maintenance, and related costs and expenses. This right is intended to give Grantors a beneficial interest in the property and to ensure that Grantors do not lose eligibility for any State homestead tax exemption for which either Grantor may otherwise qualify.

D. **DEATH OR INCAPACITY OF EITHER GRANTOR.** If either Grantor dies or becomes incapacitated, physically or mentally, to where Grantor cannot manage this Trust and whether or not a court has declared the Grantor incompetent or in need of conservator or guardian, the other spouse will serve as sole Trustee of all Trust, including any Child's Trust created under this Declaration.

E. **INCAPACITY OF BOTH GRANTORS.** The Successor Trustee must pay Trust income at least annually to, or for the benefit of, the Grantors and may also spend any amount of Trust income or Trust principal necessary, in the Successor Trustee's discretion, for the needs of the Grantors, until the Grantors, or either of them, are again able to manage their own affairs, or until their deaths. If both Grantors become physically or mentally incapacitated and are no longer able to manage this Trust, the person or persons named as Successor Trustee will serve as

Trustee. The determination of the Grantors' capacity to manage this Trust will be made by _____

_____,

who is/are reasonably available when the Successor Trustee (or any of them, if two or more are named to serve together) requests their opinion. If a majority of these persons state, in writing, that in their opinion the Grantors are no longer reasonably capable of serving as Trustee, the successor Trustee will serve as Trustee.

F. **INCAPACITY OF SURVIVING SPOUSE.** If, after the death of the Deceased Spouse, the Surviving Spouse becomes physically or mentally incapacitated and is no longer able to manage Trust B, the person or persons named as Successor Trustee will serve as Trustee.

   1) The determination of the Grantor's capacity to manage the Trust will be made by _____,
   who is/are reasonably available when the Successor Trustee (or any of them, if two or more are named to serve together) requests their opinion. If a majority of these persons state, in writing, that in their opinion the Grantor is no longer reasonably capable of serving as Trustee, the successor Trustee will serve as Trustee.

   2) The Successor Trustee will pay Trust income at least annually to or for the benefit of the Surviving Spouse and spend any amount of that Trust's principal necessary in the Successor Trustee's discretion, for the needs of the Surviving Spouse, until the Surviving Spouse is no longer incapacitated or death of the Surviving Spouse. Any income in excess of amounts spent for the benefit of the Surviving Spouse will be accumulated and added to the property of Trust B.

   3) The Successor Trustee will manage Trust A, under the terms of this Declaration, until the Surviving Spouse is able to serve as Trustee of that Trust or until the death of the Surviving Spouse.

4) The Successor Trustee will manage any operational child's Trust created by this Declaration.

G. SIMULTANEOUS DEATH OF THE GRANTORS. If both Grantors die simultaneously, or under such circumstances as to make it difficult or impossible to determine who predeceased the other, it will conclusively be presumed that both died at the same moment, and neither Grantor will be presumed to have survived the other, and the Trusts in this Declaration will become irrevocable. The Trustee will distribute the Trust property to the named beneficiaries.

4. TRUSTEES.

A. TRUSTEES. The Trustees are identified in Section 1. Establishment of Trust. Either Grantor may act as Trustee of any of the Trusts in this Declaration. The singular "Trustee" also includes the plural.

B. SUCCESSOR TRUSTEES. Upon the death or incapacity (as defined in Section 3.D. and Section 3.E.) of the surviving spouse, the "SUCCESSOR TRUSTEES" will be _____, and the Successor Trustees will become the Trustees at that time. If the Successor Trustees are not able to serve or continue serve as successor trustee, then the alternate Successor Trustees will be _____. Successor Trustees:

_____ will have the complete and independent authority to act for and represent the Trust.

[OR] [Select only one]

_____ must all consent, in writing, to any transaction involving the Trust or Trust property.

C. TRUSTEES' RESPONSIBILITY. The Trustees will serve as Trustees of all of the Trusts created in this Declaration, including any Child's Trust.

D. TRUSTEES RESIGNATION. Any Trustees may resign at any time by signing a notice of resignation and must deliver the notice of registration to the alternate Trustees under Section 4.B.

E. POWERS AND DUTIES.

1) **POWERS TO APPOINT SUCCESSOR TRUSTEES.** If the entire successor Trustees named in this Declaration, Section 4.B. cease to, or are unable to, serve as Trustees, any Trustees may appoint an additional Trustees or Successor Trustees to serve in the order nominated. The appointment must be made in writing, signed by the Trustees, and notarized.

2) **SPECIFIC DUTIES.** The Trustees' powers include, but are not limited to, the power to:

1. sell Trust property, and borrow money and to encumber Trust property, including mortgage, deed by trust, or otherwise any Trust real estate.

2. manage Trust real estate as if the Trustees were the absolute owner, including the power to lease (even lease terms that extend beyond the period of the Trust), grant options to lease Trust real estate, make repairs or alterations, and to insure against loss.

3. sell or grant options for the sale or exchange of any Trust property, including stocks, bonds, debentures, and any other form of security or security account, at public or private sale for cash or credit.

4. invest Trust property in property of any kind, including, but not limited to, bonds, debentures, notes, mortgages, stocks, stock options, stock futures, and buying on margin.

5. receive additional property from any source and add to any Trust created by this Declaration.

6. employ and pay reasonable fees to accountants, lawyers, or investment experts for information or advice relating to the Trust.

7. deposit and hold Trust funds in both interest-bearing and non-interest-bearing accounts.

8. deposit funds in bank or other accounts insured or uninsured by the FDIC.

9. enter into electronic fund transfer or safe deposit arrangements with financial institutions.

10. continue any business of the Grantors.

11. institute or defend legal actions concerning the Trust or Grantors' affairs.

12. execute any document necessary to administer any Child's Trust created in this Declaration.

13. diversify investments, including authority to decide that some or all of the Trust property need not produce income.

3) **PAYMENT OF DEBTS AND TAXES.**

1. **WIFE.** The Wife's debts and death taxes are to be paid by the Trustees from the following Trust property: _____

   _____.

   If the property is not sufficient to pay all of the Wife's debts and death taxes, then the Trustees must make a determination as to how such debts and death taxes will be paid from other Trust property.

2. **HUSBAND.** The Husband's debts and death taxes are to be paid by the Trustees from the following Trust property: _____ _____. If the property is not sufficient to pay all of the Husband's debts and death taxes, then the Trustees must make a determination as to how such debts and death taxes will be paid from other Trust property.

4) **ACCOUNTING.** No accountings or similar reports are required by Trustees for any Trust including Trust A and Trust B, except the final beneficiaries of Trust A and Trust B must be provided with copies of the annual Federal income tax return.

F. **NO TRUSTEES BOND REQUIRED.** No bond is required of any Trustees.

G. **NO TRUSTEES COMPENSATION.** No Trustees are to receive any compensation in any form for serving as Trustees, except that Trustees may be entitled to reasonable compensation, as determined by the Trustees, for serving as Trustees of a Child's Trust created by this Declaration, or for serving as Trustees if the Grantors are incapacitated.

H. **TRUSTEE LIABILITY.** With respect to the exercise or non-exercise of discretionary powers granted by this Declaration, the Trustee is not liable for actions taken in good faith.

5. **BENEFICIARIES.**

A. **WIFE'S PRIMARY AND ALTERNATE BENEFICIARIES.** On the Wife's death, Trust property owned by Wife, as her share of the Trust property listed on **Schedule A** and any separate property listed on **Schedule B** are to be distributed as specified to the beneficiaries named in this Section.

    1)   **WIFE'S SPECIFIC BENEFICIARIES.**

      1. The property identified as _____

_____

is left in Trust to_____

_____, the primary beneficiary.

If the primary beneficiary does not survive Grantors, or rejects the property, then to _____,

the alternate beneficiary.

      2. The property identified as _____

_____

is left in Trust to_____

_____, the primary beneficiary.

If the primary beneficiary does not survive Grantors, or rejects the property, then to _____,

the alternate beneficiary.

3. The property identified as _____

_____

is left in Trust to_____

_____, the primary beneficiary.

If the primary beneficiary does not survive Grantors, or rejects the

property, then to _____,

the alternate beneficiary.

B. HUSBAND'S PRIMARY AND ALTERNATE BENEFICIARIES. On the

Husband's death, Trust property owned by Husband, as his share of the Trust

property listed on **Schedule A** and any separate property listed on **Schedule C** are

to be distributed as specified to the beneficiaries named in this Section.

    1)   **HUSBAND'S SPECIFIC BENEFICIARIES.**

1. The property identified as _____

_____

is left in Trust to_____

_____, the primary beneficiary.

If the primary beneficiary does not survive Grantors, or rejects the

property, then to _____,

the alternate beneficiary.

2. The property identified as _____

_____

is left in Trust to_____

_____, the primary beneficiary.

If the primary beneficiary does not survive Grantors, or rejects the

property, then to _____,

the alternate beneficiary.

3. The property identified as _____

_____

is left in Trust to_____

_____, the primary beneficiary. If the primary beneficiary does not survive Grantors, or rejects the property, then to _____, the alternate beneficiary.

C. REMAINING TRUST PROPERTY. Except as provided by Section 5.A. or 5.B., all other Trust property of the Deceased Spouse will be transferred to, and administered as part of, Trust A, The Marital Life Estate Trust, defined in Section 6.

6. CREATION OF TRUST A ON DEATH OF DEACEASED SPOUSE.

A. TERMINOLOGY.

1) The first Grantor to die will be called the "DECEASED SPOUSE," and the living Grantor called the "SURVIVING SPOUSE."

2) "TRUST PROPERTY OF THE DECEASED SPOUSE" will contain all the property in the Trust owned by the Deceased Spouse at the time it was transferred to the Trustee, plus shared ownership property with a total value equal to one-half of the total value at the time of the Deceased Spouse's death of shared ownership property, plus accumulated income, appreciation in value, and the like, attributable to the ownership interest of the Deceased Spouse, and his or her share of all property acquired in the Trust's or Trustees' names.

3) "TRUST PROPERTY OF THE SURVIVING SPOUSE" will contain all the property in the Trust owned by the Surviving Spouse at the time it was transferred to the Trustee, plus shared ownership property with a total value equal to one-half of the total value at the time of the Deceased Spouse's death of shared ownership property, plus accumulated income, appreciation in value, and the like, attributable to the ownership interest of the Deceased Spouse, and his or her share of all property acquired in the Trust's or Trustees' names plus any property acquired under the terms of this Trust.

B. DEATH OF SPOUSE TRUST PROPERTY DIVISION DISTRIBUTION.

1) DISCLAIMER TRUST

_____ **NO DISCLAIMER TRUST** (Go to 6.C. Administration of Trust A.)

[OR] [select only one]

_____ **DISCLAIMER TRUST**, as follows:

1. After the death of the Deceased Spouse, the Trustee must divide the Trust assets into three shares, called the Survivor's Share, the Marital Deduction Share, and the Bypass Trust Share.

   a. **SURVIVOR'S SHARE.** This share consists of the Trust assets of the Surviving Spouse, as defined in Section 6.A.3. These assets will be held in and administered as part of Trust B, the Surviving Spouse's Trust.

   b. **MARITAL DEDUCTION SHARE.** This share consists of the assets that pass to the Surviving Spouse under this Declaration that are not disclaimed by the Surviving Spouse within nine months of the Deceased Spouse's death. These assets will be held in and administered as part of Trust B.

   c. **THE BYPASS TRUST SHARE.** This share consists of assets that pass to the Surviving Spouse under this Declaration that are disclaimed by the Surviving Spouse. The assets will be held and administered in Trust A, the Deceased Spouse's Trust.

2. **DISCLAIMER OF TRUST ASSETS.** The Surviving Spouse has the authority to disclaim any Trust assets left to him or her by the Deceased Spouse. The Surviving Spouse is not required to disclaim any of these Trust assets. If the Surviving Spouse chooses

to disclaim property, they will do so within nine months after the Deceased Spouse's death. Any disclaimed property will be called the "Bypass Trust Share," and will be held and administered in Trust A. If the Surviving Spouse does not disclaim any assets left to him or her by the Deceased Spouse's Trust, the Trustee shall not establish Trust A.

2)   On the death of the Deceased Spouse, the Trustee will divide the Trust property listed on Schedules A, B, and C into two separate trusts, Trust A and Trust B.

3)   All Trust property of the Deceased Spouse, as defined in Section 6.A.2., will be placed in a trust known as Trust A, after making any specific gifts provided for in Section 5.A. or 5.B., subject to any provision in this Declaration that creates child's trusts or creates custodianship under the Uniform Transfers to Minors Act.

4)   The Trustee will place all Trust property of the Surviving Spouse, as defined in Section 6.A.3., in a trust known as Trust B (The Surviving Spouse's Trust).

5)   Physical segregation of the property in any Trust is not required to divide that Trust's property into Trust A and Trust B. The Trustee will exclusively determine what records, documents, and actions are required to establish and maintain Trust A and Trust B.

C. ADMINISTRATION OF TRUST A. All property held in Trust A will be administered as follows:

1)   Trust A becomes irrevocable at the death of the Deceased Spouse.

2)   Trust A's life beneficiary is the Surviving Spouse.

3)   If Wife is the Deceased Spouse, then the final beneficiaries of Trust A will be: _____

_____,

and the alternate final beneficiaries of Trust A will be: _____

_____.

4) If Husband is the Deceased Spouse, then the final beneficiaries of Trust A will be: _____

_____, and the alternate final beneficiaries of Trust A will be: _____

_____.

5) The Trustee will be entitled to reasonable compensation from assets of Trust A for services rendered managing Trust A, without court approval.

6) On the death of the life beneficiary, the Trustee must distribute the property of Trust A to the final beneficiary or beneficiaries, as named in Section 6.C.3 or 6.C.4.

7. **CREATION OF TRUST B THE SURVIVING SPOUSE'S TRUST. Upon the death** of the Deceased Spouse, all Trust property owned by the Surviving Spouse, as defined in Section 6.A.3., will be held in Trust B, The Surviving Spouse's Trust. Trust B will include any Trust property of the Deceased Spouse left to the Surviving Spouse and not disclaimed by them.

   A. **ADMINISTRATION OF TRUST B.** Until the death of the Surviving Spouse, the Surviving Spouse retains all rights to all income, profits, and control of the property in Trust B. The Surviving Spouse may amend or revoke Trust B at any time during their lifetime, without notifying any beneficiary.

   B. **DISTRIBUTION OF PROPERTY IN TRUSTB.**

   1) On the death of the Surviving Spouse, Trust B becomes irrevocable.

   2) The Trustee will first distribute any Specific Gifts of the Surviving Spouse to the beneficiaries. The Trustee will then distribute all remaining property of Trust B to their final or alternate final beneficiaries.

   3) All distributions regarding Trust B are subject to any provision in this Declaration that creates child's Trusts or creates custodianships under the Uniform Transfers to Minors Act.

8. **AMENDING AB TRUST WHEN ESTATE TAX LAWS CHANGE.** If the U.S. Congress changes the estate tax law, this Trust may be amended as follows:

   A. If both Grantors are alive, but one is incapacitated, the competent spouse may amend this AB Trust in order to take best advantage of the new tax law.

   B. If both Grantors are alive, but incapacitated, the Successor Trustee may amend this AB Trust in order to take best advantage of the new tax law.

9. **CHILD(REN)'S SUBTRUST(S).** All Trust property left to any of the minor or young adult beneficiaries listed below in Section 6.A. will be retained in Trust for each named child beneficiary in a separate Trust that can be identified and referred to by adding the name of that Trust's beneficiary to the name of this Trust. The following terms apply to each Child's Trust:

   A. **TRUST BENEFICIARIES AND AGE LIMITS.** A Child's Trust ends when the beneficiary of that Trust becomes 35, except as otherwise specified in this Section:

   Trust for   Ends at Age

   _____   _____

   _____   _____

   _____   _____

   B. **TRUSTEES POWERS AND DUTIES.**

   1)   Until a Child's Trust ends, the Trustees may distribute or use assets for the benefit of the beneficiary as the Trustees deems necessary for the beneficiary's health, support, maintenance, or education. Education includes, but is not limited to, college, graduate, professional, and vocational studies, and reasonably related living expenses.

   2)   In deciding whether to make a distribution to the beneficiary, the

Trustees may take into account the beneficiary's other income, resources, and sources of support.

3)   Any Child's Trust income that is not distributed to a beneficiary by the Trustees will accumulate and add to the principal of the Trust for that beneficiary.

4)   The Trustees of a Child's Trust is not required to make any accounting or report to the Trust beneficiary.

C. **NO ASSIGNMENT OF BENEFICIARY INTEREST.** The interests of the beneficiary of a Child's Trust cannot be transferred by voluntary or involuntary assignment or by operation of law before actual receipt by the beneficiary. These interests are free from the claims of creditors and from attachments, execution, bankruptcy, or other legal process to the fullest extent permitted by law.

D. **TRUSTEES COMPENSATION.** Any Trustees of a Child's Trust created under this Declaration will be entitled to reasonable compensation out of the Trust assets for ordinary and extraordinary services, and for all services in connection with the termination of any Trust.

E. **TERMINATION.** A Child's Trust will end when any of the following events occur:

1)   the beneficiary reaches the age specified in Section 6.A. If the Trust ends for this reason, the remaining principal and accumulated income of the Trust will be given outright to the beneficiary.

2)   the beneficiary dies. If the Trust ends for this reason, the Trust property will pass to the beneficiary's heirs.

3)   the Trustees distribute all Trust property under the provisions of this Declaration.

F. **CUSTODIANSHIPS UNDER THE UNIFORM TRANSFERS TO MINORS ACT.**

1)   All property _____

beneficiary becomes entitled to under this Trust is given to _____

_____to act as custodian for _____

_____under the State of _____

_____Uniform Transfers to Minors Act, until the beneficiary reaches age

_____.

    2)   All property _____,

beneficiary becomes entitled to under this Trust is given to _____

_____to act as custodian for _____

_____under the State of _____

_____Uniform Transfers to Minors Act, until the beneficiary reaches age

_____.

    3)   All property _____,

beneficiary becomes entitled to under this Trust is given to _____

_____to act as custodian for _____

_____under the State of _____

_____Uniform Transfers to Minors Act, until the beneficiary reaches age

_____.

    4)   All property _____,

beneficiary becomes entitled to under this Trust is given to _____

_____to act as custodian for _____

_____under the State of _____

_____Uniform Transfers to Minors Act, until the beneficiary reaches age

_____.

10. CERTIFICATION BY GRANTORS. I certify that I have read this Declaration and that it correctly states the terms and conditions under which the Trust property is to be held, managed, and disposed of by the Trustees, and I approve the Declaration.

_____   _____

Grantors and Trustees, Wife   Date

_____   _____

Grantors and Trustees, Husband   Date

NOTARY PUBLIC ACKNOWLEDGEMENT

The foregoing instrument was acknowledged, subscribed, and sworn to before me,

_____this _____day of _____, 20_____, personally known to me (or proved to me on the basis of satisfactory evidence) to be the person whose name is subscribed to the foregoing instrument, and acknowledged to me that he or she executed the same in his or her authorized capacity and that by his or her signature on the instrument, the person, or the entity upon behalf of which the person acted, executed the instrument.

Witness my hand and official seal.

_____

NOTARY PUBLIC for the State of _____

My Commission Expires: _____

[For Notary Seal or Stamp]

_____

NOTARY PUBLIC

Schedule A—Shared Property Placed in Trust

All the grantor's interest in the following property: _____

_____

_____

_____

_____

_____

_____

_____

_____

_____

_____

_____

_____

_____

_____

_____

_____

_____

_____

_____

_____

Schedule B—Wife's Separate Property Placed in Trust

All of Wife's interest in the following property: _____

_____

_____

_____

_____

_____

_____

_____

_____

_____

_____

_____

_____

_____

_____

_____

_____

_____

_____

_____

_____

_____

Schedule C—Husband's Separate Property Placed in Trust

All of Husband's interest in the following property: _____

_____

_____

_____

_____

_____

_____

_____

_____

_____

_____

_____

_____

_____

_____

_____

_____

_____

_____

_____

_____

FLORIDA WITNESS STATEMENT FOR LIVING TRUSTS

On this _____ day of _____, 20____, _____

declared to me, the undersigned, under penalty of perjury that the person who signed or acknowledged the living trust was their living trust, called the Declaration of Trust dated _____ day of _____, 20_____, requested me to act as witness to their hand in signing the document in my presence, and did so in my presence. I sign my name being first duly sworn and do declare that the signatures of the Declaration of Trust mentioned above was signed willingly, or willingly directed by another to sign for him/her, and that I, sign below as witness and to the best of my knowledge all parties are eighteen years of age or older, of sound mind and under no constraint or undue influence.

_____   _____
Witness's Signature   Printed Name of Witness

_____
Address of Witness

ASSIGNMENT OF PROPERTY TO A LIVING TRUST

I/We _____and _____,

Grantor(s), and Trustee(s) of the Living Trust, dated _____, assign and

transfer all rights, title, and interest in the following property: _____

_____

_____

_____

_____

_____

_____

_____

_____

_____

I/We execute this Assignment of Property on the _____day of _____, 20____
and declare, under penalty of perjury of the law, that I am/we are signing and executing this
document willingly, under my/our own free and voluntary act, and that I am/we are of the age of
majority or otherwise legally empowered to make this document and under no constraint or
undue influence.

_____   _____
Grantor and Trustee Signature   Printed Name of Grantor and Trustee

_____
Address of Grantor and Trustee

_____   _____
Grantor and Trustee Signature   Printed Name of Grantor and Trustee

_____
Address of Grantor and Trustee

NOTARY PUBLIC ACKNOWLEDGEMENT

The foregoing instrument was acknowledged, subscribed, and sworn to before me,

_____this _____day of _____, 20____, personally known to me (or proved to me on the basis of satisfactory evidence) to be the person whose name is subscribed to the foregoing instrument, and acknowledged to me that he or she executed the same in his or her authorized capacity and that by his or her signature on the instrument, the person, or the entity upon behalf of which the person acted, executed the instrument.

Witness my hand and official seal.

_____

NOTARY PUBLIC for the State of _____

My Commission Expires: _____

[For Notary Seal or Stamp]

_____

NOTARY PUBLIC

AFFIDAVIT OF ASSUMPTION OF DUTIES BY SUCCESSOR TRUSTEE

I, _____, Successor Trustee whose address is ____

_____City _____,

County_____, State _____, being of legal age

and first being duly sworn, declare:

On the ____day of _____, 20____, Grantor(s) _____

and _____created a Living Trust with them as Grantor(s).

On the ____day of _____, 20____, Grantor _____

died, and on the ____day of _____, 20____, the other Grantor _____

_____died. A certified copy of the Certificate of Death is/are attached. The Declaration of Trust creating the Living Trust provides that upon the death of the Grantors, I,

_____become the Trustee of the Trust.

I hereby accept the office of Trustee of the Trust, and I am from this time forward acting as Trustee of the Trust.

Successor Trustee signature _____Date: _____

NOTARY PUBLIC ACKNOWLEDGEMENT

The foregoing instrument was acknowledged, subscribed, and sworn to before me,

_____this ____day of _____, 20____,

personally known to me (or proved to me on the basis of satisfactory evidence) to be the person whose name is subscribed to the foregoing instrument, and acknowledged to me that they executed the same in their authorized capacity and that by their signature on the instrument, the person, or the entity upon behalf of which the person acted, executed the instrument. Witness my hand and official seal.

NOTARY PUBLIC for the State of _____County of _____

My Commission Expires: _____

[For Notary Seal or Stamp]

LIVING TRUST AMENDMENT

I/We _____ and _____,

as Grantor(s) and Trustee(s) of the Living Trust dated _____ make the following Amendments as allowed by the Living Trust:

1) Changes to the Living Trust: _____

_____

_____

_____

2) Add to the Living Trust: _____

_____

_____

_____

3) In all other respects we confirm and republish the Living Trust dated _____

as modified by this Amendment.

I/We subscribe to this Amendment this day _____ of _____, 20_____, and declare, under penalty of perjury of the law, that I/we sign and execute this document willingly, under my/our own free and voluntary act and that I am/we are of the age of majority or otherwise legally empowered to make this document and am/are under no constraint or undue influence.

_____   _____
Grantor and Trustee Signature   Printed Name of Grantor and Trustee

_____   _____
Address of Grantor and Trustee

_____   _____
Grantor and Trustee Signature   Printed Name of Grantor and Trustee

_____   _____
Address of Grantor and Trustee

NOTARY PUBLIC ACKNOWLEDGEMENT

The foregoing instrument was acknowledged, subscribed, and sworn to before me,

_____this _____day of _____, 20____, personally known to me (or proved to me on the basis of satisfactory evidence) to be the person whose name is subscribed to the foregoing instrument, and acknowledged to me that he or she executed the same in his or her authorized capacity and that by his or her signature on the instrument, the person, or the entity upon behalf of which the person acted, executed the instrument.

Witness my hand and official seal.

_____

NOTARY PUBLIC for the State of _____

My Commission Expires: _____

[For Notary Seal or Stamp]

_____

NOTARY PUBLIC

REVOCATION OF LIVING TRUST

I/We, _____, whose address is _____

_____ City_____

County _____State _____, revoke the Living Will

dated _____, in its entirety without limitations, including revoking any
appointment of any persons named in the above Living Trust. Under the terms of the Living
Trust, the Grantor(s) reserved the power to revoke the Trust. Under these terms, and the laws of
the State of _____, the Grantor(s) revoke the Living Trust and state the Trust is
completely revoked. All property of the Trust will be returned to the Grantor(s) and legally
owned by the original Grantor(s) as defined in the Trust.

Grantor and Trustee signature: _____Date: _____

Grantor and Trustee signature: _____Date: _____

NOTARY PUBLIC ACKNOWLEDGEMENT

The foregoing instrument was acknowledged, subscribed, and sworn to before me,

_____this _____day of _____,

20_____,personally known to me (or proved to me on the basis of satisfactory evidence) to be the
person whose name is subscribed to the foregoing instrument, and acknowledged to me that he or
she executed the same in his or her authorized capacity and that by his or her signature on the
instrument, the person, or the entity upon behalf of which the person acted, executed the
instrument.

Witness my hand and official seal.

_____

NOTARY PUBLIC for the State of _____

My Commission Expires: _____

[For Notary Seal or Stamp]

_____
NOTARY PUBLIC

VI. You Created Your Legal Document, Now What?

1. Storing Your Documents

Now that you have created your legal documents, you need to store them. You will also need to know how to make any necessary changes. Most of the rules governing wills, also applies to trusts and powers of attorney. In this chapter, you will learn how to store and make changes to your legal documents.

A. Where to Keep It

Your legal documents should be easy for your executor and/or trustees to find and at least one other person. The people you entrust with the location of your legal documents do not need to know their contents or who you named as beneficiaries.

Generally, people store all of their legal documents together in their safety deposit box at a bank or in their house safe. These are both excellent places to store your legal documents because, if the executor or trustees do not know where your legal documents are, the safety deposit box or the house safe is a likely place they will look for the documents.

There is no legal requirement for where you should store your legal documents. That is entirely up to you.

B. How to Keep It

When you store your legal documents, you can staple the pages together along with any self-proving affidavits and/or any other documents that you want to be distributed after you die and place them in a larger envelope with "Estate Documents" written on the envelope. You may want to put your power of attorney and/or living will in a separate envelope because these documents are only effective while you are still alive.

C. Making Copies

Copying your legal documents is practical, but the copies are not legally binding without your original signatures, the signatures of your witnesses, and/or notarizations. Probate courts require originals. While the copy you make might not be legally binding, you may still want to give a copy for your executor to help them prepare for their duties.

If you make a copy of your will before it is signed, witnessed, and notarized, and *then* have all of the wills (the original and the copy) executed to be valid wills, most states allow you to have multiple, valid wills so long as they are the same. It is not advisable to do so, however, because:

- if you need to revoke your will, you will need to revoke every copy out there and they may not be easy to track down, or
- if you forget that you made duplicates and need to later revoke your will, you may have some forgotten open provisions.

A financial durable power of attorney copy may be accepted by third parties.

2. Making Changes to Your Existing Documents

Every few years, periodically, you should review your legal documents and make any changes to reflect the property that you have acquired or changes to your life. Also, this can give you a chance to make sure that your wishes have not changed.

A. Changes in Life

You should update your legal documents following changes in your life. These events include:

- changes to your marital status such as getting married, divorced, or remarried,
- birth or adoption of children, from current or previous marriage(s), or grandchildren,
- death of a parent, spouse, child, or anyone named in your legal documents,
- significant financial losses, gains, or the addition of new debts,
- changing your state of residence, or
- buying property in another state.

B. How to Make Changes

Changes to your legal documents, made after the documents have been signed notarized and/or witnessed, can be done by including a statement that supersedes all prior documents. A statement that you put in your new legal documents that supersedes the previous one is known as a *codicil or an amendment*. Generally, it is best to add a codicil that rejects all prior

documents and makes your changes in a new document.

C. Consequences of Not Making Changes

Failure to change your documents after significant life events can have unintended consequences. For example, if the people in your will are now all dead, then your will would pass according to state law, which usually means your property would pass to your relatives, and your wishes might not be fulfilled. If you have children after you create your legal documents, and no children are named in the documents because your legal documents have not been updated, then the court may end up deciding who will care for your minor children. Your estate will also have to spend the added cost of litigation for disputes of unsettled matters that are not addressed in your legal documents.

D. Revoke an Existing Legal Document

For a will, in addition to being revocable by codicil or, in special cases, by holographic will, you can also revoke the will be physical action. Physical action means tearing, burning, or, in some other way, physically destroying the will. Simply scratching out the names on your will is generally not enough.

Physically destroying any of the other legal documents will have no effect on their legality. To revoke these other legal documents, you will need to enter into a separate codicil that revokes the documents.

E. Reviving a Revoked Legal Document

When you destroy a second will by a physical action that had previously revoked a first will, the first will is not revived by your physical destruction of your second will. It is bad practice to try to do so. You can, however, create a third will that contains the same, or similar, information.

For any legal document that you revoke by codicil, no prior versions of the legal document are revived automatically. To revive an earlier version, you would need to create a third document that contains your needs.

F. If a Legal Document Is Missing At Death

If your will cannot be found at the time you die, the probate court will assume that the will has been revoked. Also, if there is a valid first will that was revoked by the missing second will, then the first will is legally valid because, remember, a will is not binding until it has been approved by a probate court. Therefore, all previous wills, that are revoked, should be physically destroyed to avoid this kind of problem and confusion.

For a living trust, you are allowed to have more than one valid living trust. If trust documents are missing, evidence can be provided of the trust's existence.

For all other documents, if the documents cannot be found when they are needed and/or at your death, then that signals to the court or third parties that the documents have been revoked.

VII.   Additional Resources

1.   Attorney

While you are creating your legal documents, or even after you have created them, you may need additional resource. In this chapter, you will learn about retaining an attorney.

A.   Hiring an Attorney

If you think you can simply complete the sample forms in this book and have an attorney look them over for you, you may have a hard time finding an attorney that will take on the job. Even if you do find an attorney willing to take it on, you may find it to be more costly than having them create the documents. One reason may be the attorney is not completely comfortable with taking on someone's work on their reputation. If you decide to hire an attorney, there are some things to consider including the type of attorney, finding an attorney, and fees.

B.   Type of an Attorney to Hire

The type of attorney that you hire depends on what problem you need to solve. For estate planning you may need an attorney who specializes in estates as well as elder, tax, real estate, or business law. Your attorney, at a minimum, should be a member of your state's bar. Because the information that you provide is very personal, you should seek an attorney that you feel comfortable talking with.

C.   Finding an Attorney

There are many ways to go about finding a competent attorney. You can ask family, friends, or businesses that you respect for recommendations. Generally, you can go to an attorney that you have been referred to even if they do not practice in estate planning. They may take you as a client, or they may refer you to someone who can. You can search online on an established online directory that allows you to narrow your search by location and practice area. However, these directories tend to list established attorneys with high fees. If you are part of a group legal plan as part of a union, employer, or consumer group, you might start with them and get your problems taken care of for free or at a reduced rate.

D.   Attorney Fees

Attorneys can be expensive. Fees commonly range from $150 to $500 per hour, or more. But, the high cost does not always translate into better service. You are better off with an attorney that understands your unique situation. Fees should be disclosed upfront and you should make sure to get something affirmative in writing. If you agree to a set price for the work to be completed, you should know what the conditions are which can change that contract price or other terms.

2. Legal Research

Doing your own legal research is a challenge because you may not know where to even go to look for resources. Even where you find information you may not know if the information you are finding is correct or up to date. For these reasons, and more, we do not recommend that you rely solely on your own legal research.

A. Law Libraries

Going to a law library and searching online can serve as a useful starting point. Most law school libraries are Federal repositories and therefore are open to the public during normal business hours. While at the law library, librarians are usually happy to help you find information and provide you with some guidance about where to begin your research. Some public libraries have some legal books that may be useful. Also, your local county courthouse may have a law library, however, selections vary.

B. Online

It is possible to find quality information online. You personally have to gauge, not only the reputation of the information that you are being presented, but also the date of the information. If you go to a law library, a librarian may recommend some online tools as well as some printed materials.

Appendix

State Specific Information

Alabama:
PeerlessLegal.com/wtpo/al-alabama/
Alaska:
PeerlessLegal.com/wtpo/ak-alaska/
Arizona:
PeerlessLegal.com/wtpo/az-arizona/
Arkansas:
PeerlessLegal.com/wtpo/ar-arkansas/
California:
PeerlessLegal.com/wtpo/ca-california/
Colorado:
PeerlessLegal.com/wtpo/co-colorado/
Connecticut:
PeerlessLegal.com/wtpo/ct-connecticut/
Delaware:
PeerlessLegal.com/wtpo/de-delaware/
District of Columbia, Washington:
PeerlessLegal.com/wtpo/dc-washington/
Florida:
PeerlessLegal.com/wtpo/fl-florida/
Georgia:
PeerlessLegal.com/wtpo/ga-georgia/
Hawaii:
PeerlessLegal.com/wtpo/hi-hawaii/
Idaho:
PeerlessLegal.com/wtpo/id-idaho/
Illinois:
PeerlessLegal.com/wtpo/il-illinois/
Indiana:
PeerlessLegal.com/wtpo/in-indiana/
Iowa:
PeerlessLegal.com/wtpo/ia-iowa/
Kansas:
PeerlessLegal.com/wtpo/ks-kansas/
Kentucky:
PeerlessLegal.com/wtpo/ky-kentucky/
Louisiana:
PeerlessLegal.com/wtpo/la-louisiana/
Maine:
PeerlessLegal.com/wtpo/me-maine/

Maryland:
PeerlessLegal.com/wtpo/md-maryland/
Massachusetts:
PeerlessLegal.com/wtpo/ma-massachusetts/
Michigan:
PeerlessLegal.com/wtpo/mi-michigan/
Minnesota:
PeerlessLegal.com/wtpo/mn-minnesota/
Mississippi:
PeerlessLegal.com/wtpo/ms-mississippi/
Missouri:
PeerlessLegal.com/wtpo/mo-missouri/
Montana:
PeerlessLegal.com/wtpo/mt-montana/
Nebraska:
PeerlessLegal.com/wtpo/ne-nebraska/
Nevada:
PeerlessLegal.com/wtpo/nv-nevada/
New Hampshire:
PeerlessLegal.com/wtpo/nh-new-hampshire/
New Jersey:
PeerlessLegal.com/wtpo/nj-new-jersey/
New Mexico:
PeerlessLegal.com/wtpo/nm-new-mexico/
New York:
PeerlessLegal.com/wtpo/ny-new-york/
North Carolina:
PeerlessLegal.com/wtpo/nc-north-carolina/
North Dakota:
PeerlessLegal.com/wtpo/nd-north-dakota/
Ohio:
PeerlessLegal.com/wtpo/oh-ohio/
Oklahoma:
PeerlessLegal.com/wtpo/ok-oklahoma/
Oregon:
PeerlessLegal.com/wtpo/or-oregon/
Pennsylvania:
PeerlessLegal.com/wtpo/pa-pennsylvania/

Rhode Island:
PeerlessLegal.com/wtpo/ri-rhode-island/
South Carolina:
PeerlessLegal.com/wtpo/sc-south-carolina/
South Dakota:
PeerlessLegal.com/wtpo/sd-south-dakota/
Tennessee:
PeerlessLegal.com/wtpo/tn-tennessee/
Texas:
PeerlessLegal.com/wtpo/tx-texas/
Utah:
PeerlessLegal.com/wtpo/ut-utah/

Vermont:
PeerlessLegal.com/wtpo/vt-vermont/
Virginia:
PeerlessLegal.com/wtpo/va-virginia/
Washington (State):
PeerlessLegal.com/wtpo/wa-washington/
West Virginia:
PeerlessLegal.com/wtpo/wv-west-virginia/
Wisconsin:
PeerlessLegal.com/wtpo/wi-wisconsin/
Wyoming:
PeerlessLegal.com/wtpo/wy-wyoming/

Glossary

AB Trust. Spousal tax saving estate trust where the surviving spouse leaves property in "Trust A" and allows the spouse use of the property during the spouse's lifetime, and authorizes limited rights to invade the trust principal. After the surviving spouse's death, the trust property goes to the beneficiaries.

AB Disclaimer Trust. Similar to an AB Trust, the surviving spouse decides how much, if any, of deceased spouse property will be places in Trust A.

Acknowledgement. A statement in front of a person qualified to administer an oath (notary public) that a document with a person's signature was actually signed by the person claimed on the document.

Administration of an Estate. A court supervised distribution of the probate estate of decedent. The manager of the distribution is the executor if there is a will, and if there is not will, then this person is called an administrator. In a few states the personal representative takes either one of these roles.

Administrator. Someone not named in the decedent's will and acts as a personal representative.

Adult. Generally, someone that is over the age of 18.

Affidavit. A written statement that is signed under oath in front of a notary public.

Alternate Beneficiary. If a primary beneficiary dies before the person who creates the will or trust does, then the property will pass to the alternate beneficiary.

Augmented Estate. Property left by will plus certain property transferred outside of the will by gifts, joint tenancies, and living trusts. Augmented estates are calculated if a surviving spouse wants to claim their statutory share of the deceased spouse's property. A surviving spouse is considered to be adequately provided for it they receive at least one-third of the augmented estate.

Basis. A tax term dealing with valuation of property for determining profit or loss on sale. Example, if you buy a house for $100,000, then your basis will be $100,000. If you sell your house for $150,000, then your taxable profit will be $50,000.

Beneficiary. The named recipient of an asset belonging to a decedent in a will or trust.

Bequest. A gift that becomes effective at the time of death.

Bond. Monetary guarantees that an estate, a trust, or a custodianship from the dishonest acts of a fiduciary.

Bypass Trust. Also called an AB Trust.

Certification. In the presence of a notary public who acknowledges you signing and dating a living trust.

Child's Trust. A trust created for a young beneficiary that has not reached the age specified by the grantor (can be greater than 18 years of age) or age 35, whichever comes first.

Codicil. An amendment to a will.

Common Law Marriage. Only in a handful of states, a common law marriage is where the state recognizes a couple as being married if they have lived together for a certain amount of time and intent to be husband and wife.

Community Property. Any and all property acquired during a marriage from the efforts of one or both of the spouses. Only used in Arizona, California, Idaho, Louisiana, Nevada, New Mexico, Texas, Washington (State), and Wisconsin.

Conservator. Appointed by the court, it is someone who manages the affairs of a mentally incompetent person. Also called a guardian in a few states.

Creditor. Institution or person to whom money is owed.

Custodian. A person appointed under the Uniform Gift of Minors Act (also used interchangeably with the name Uniform Transfers to Minors Act), who has a fiduciary position over assets for the benefit of a minor. The custodian can use the property for the benefit of the minor child including for the minor's health, education, or other support. Court does not supervise the custodian.

Debtor. A person who owes money.

Deceased Spouse. It is the first spouse to die in a living trust or an AB Trust.

Decedent. Person who died.

Decedent's Trust. Trust created at the decedent's death to take advantage of decedent's Federal estate tax exemption.

Deed. The legal document that transfers real estate title.

Descendant. Any person born into the family line e.g., daughter, son, grandchild.

Devise. A bequest of real property and in many States is used interchangeably with bequest.

Devisee. Someone who has been left real property in a will.

Disclaimer Trust. Trust where a beneficiary has the specific right to disclaim all or any part of a gift left them in the trust, and the gift will then pass to the next in line.

Disinheritance Clause. Clause stating that all persons other than your specifically named beneficiaries are disinherited.

Domicile. The state or country of primary residence.

Donee. Someone who receives a gift.

Donor. Someone who gives a gift.

Durable Power of Attorney. A power of attorney that survives the maker's (principal) incapacity.

Estate. Generally referred to as all of the property you own on your death.

Executor. A person named in the decedent's will who will manage the decedent's estate including having the estate go through probate court, collect the assets, and distribute them. Some states call the executor the personal representative.

Execution. The act of signing a will by the testator and the witnesses.

Fiduciary. The duty to act on someone else's behalf in a fair and trustworthy manner. The person who holds this duty is also called a fiduciary.

Gift. Property given to another person or organization. This can happen after or before death, or using a will or trust.

Grantor. Same as settlor. The person who creates a trust.

Guardian. Appointed person to look after a minor and/or the minor's estate.

Heir. Entitlement of an asset of a decedent when no person is named as the beneficiary of that asset.

Holographic Will. A handwritten will by the testator of the essential terms. To be legal, the holographic will requires the testator's signature anywhere on the will (signature does not necessarily have to be at the end of the holographic will), and does not require witnesses. Not valid in all states.

Inherit. Receiving property upon the death of another.

Instrument. Legal jargon often used to refer to a document.

Inter Vivos Trust. Also called a living trust. A trust created during a lifetime (versus one created at the time of death). Generally, the trust is for the benefit of the person creating the trust, but is irrevocable on death of the creator.

Intestate. Someone who dies with no will.

Intestate Succession. Decedent's property is distributed to the decedent's heirs when there is no will or the will fails to distribute the decedent's property.

Irrevocable Trust. A trust that once created cannot be revoked or amended by the person who created it.

Issue. The lineal descendants of a person e.g., your children, grandchildren.

Joint Tenancy. Written title naming one or more persons as equal owners (called joint tenants), and upon the death of a joint tenant, the remaining joint tenants take the share of the decreased joint tenancy by right of survivorship, regardless of contrary provisions in a will. Joint tenancy is not favored by courts so creation of joint tenancy generally requires exact language. Example: A, B, and C are joint tenants in Greenacre. A dies. B and C are joint tenant is Greenacre and the heirs of A have no interest in Greenacre. The last one to outlive between B and C takes all of Greenacre.

Legacy. Gift given of personal property in a will.

Life Estate. Right given to use of property for the life a person. No right of transfer or interest is given to the property. At the death of the measuring life, the life estate ends and all interests are retained by the grantor.

Living Trust. Also called an inter vivos trust. Trust created during the life of a person, and is generally for the benefit of the person who creates the trust, but it becomes irrevocable upon the death of the person who creates the trust.

Living Will. A document that tells doctors and other healthcare professionals whether you want to have your life prolonged through artificial means such as a respirator.

Marital Property. Property acquired during a marriage from the efforts of one or more of the spouses.

Marital Trust. Trust created at death, and for the benefit off the decedent spouse to take advantage of Federal estate tax exemptions. The surviving spouse is not able to make changes to the trust.

Minor. Someone under the age of majority, generally 18 years of age.

Mortgage. A document that has a real estate as its collateral until the payment of debt is complete.

Notary Public. A person authorized by a state to administer oaths.

Payable on Death (POD). An account (often a bank account) that will pass to a designated beneficiary on the owner's death.

Personal Guardian. An adult appointed or selected to care for a minor child in the event no biological or adoptive parents take responsibility for the child.

Personal Property. Everything else that is not real estate. This would include vehicles, cash, and pets.

Pour-Over Will. Property left through the will must go through probate before it goes into the trust i.e., a will that "pours over" property into a trust.

Power of Attorney. An authorization of someone other than you to act on your behalf.

Primary Beneficiary. The person who directly inherits property in a will or trust, but does not have rights of ownership until after the death of the creator of the will or trust.

Principal. Property owned by a trust. Also used to refer to income generated by a property.

Probate Code. Statutes in almost every state that govern wills, trusts, and probate.

Probate Court. Supervised changes of titles of assets from a decedent's name to the name of the beneficiaries under the decedent's will or decedent's heirs if the decedent died without a will.

Probate Estate. All of decedent's property that passes through probate i.e., all property owned at death that is not held in joint tenancy, a living trust, a bank account trust, or in a life insurance policy.

Property Guardian. Person named in a will to take care of property given to a minor child.

Quasi-Community Property. Property that is acquired in a state that is not a community property, during a marriage, and dies in a community property state with the property being physically in the community property state; the property is treated as community property.

Real Property. Land, buildings on land, long-term leases, rights to minerals, condominiums, and co-ops. Also called real estate.

Recording. Filing a copy of a deed with the county land records office that the land sits on. This is considered a public record.

Remainder. The balances on the estate after all of the specific gifts have been distributed.

Remainderman. The person who will take the property after the life usage of the property by another e.g., if the testator bequeaths a life estate in testator's residence to A, and then at A's death, the residence will pass to B; B would be the remainderman.

Residuary Beneficiary. The beneficiary receives any property that the will creator owned at the time of death but did not leave to beneficiaries by will or otherwise.

Residue. Assets in an estate or will that are left over after distribution of all of the specific bequests.

Restatement. Restating terms of the living trust and acts as an amendment and a way of revoking the living trust.

Self-Proving Affidavit. Legal in most state, it is a document stating a witness will not be required to testify in court to prove a will offered for probate is the last will of testament of the decedent.

Self-Proving Will. Where a will is self-proving under the law of a state, then nearly all states will allow the will's admission into probate of uncontested wills without testimony of a witness to the will. In California, a will is self-proving if the witnesses attest, under penalty and perjury, that the will was property executed.

Separate Property. Property belonging entirely to one person.

Settlor. The one who creates the trust.

Successor Trustee. Person or entity (e.g., business) who serves a trustee of a trust document on the resignation, removal, or death of a trustee. For most living trusts, this is the person or entity named to act as trustee once the original trustee is no longer able to serve as trustee.

Surety Bond. A type of inexpensive insurance to guarantee the executor will act honestly; the bond is posted by the executor in an equal amount to the value of personal property in the estate (not allowed for real estate).

Survivor's Trust. Trust created after the death for the benefit of decedent's spouse to take advantage of Federal estate tax exemptions, and the surviving spouse has the power to make changes the trust.

Tenancy by the entirety. Property that is owned by married people in a state that recognizes tenancy by the entirety. The property owned and acquired during the marriage will be held as joint tenants.

Tenancy in Common. Ownership of property between two or more people to own property as co-owners but with each retaining their complete interest, including the right to leave their share of their property to their heirs.

Testate. When a person dies with no will.

Testator. The one whose will is being discussed.

Title. A document proving ownership of property.

Totten Trust. Designated assets as "in trust for" another.

Transfer on Death (TOD). Account that passes directly to a designated beneficiary on the owner's death.

Trust. Legal entity and relationship where one person or entity holds legal title and responsibility to property for the financial benefit of another person or entity.

Trustee. Person holding title to trust assets for the benefit of the beneficiary of the trust, and is responsible for management of trust assets and has a fiduciary relationship to the beneficiaries of the trust.

Uniform Gift of Minors Act. A statute adopted by most states that provides a method for transferring property to minors and arranging for an adult to manage it until the child is no longer a child (usually 18). Also goes by the name Uniform Transfers to Minors Act (UTMA).

Will. A written document created at the death of someone to direct distribution of their assets. A will is generally not going to affect assets held in joint tenancy, distributed in a contract (e.g., life insurance policy, pension, annuity.), or property subject to a payable on death or transfer on death designation.

Witnesses. Person who sees a testator sign their will and signs the will after the testator. The witness generally must be at least 18 years of age, know that the document being signed is a will, and is not entitled to anything in the will.

Index

Visit PeerlessLegal.com. Get:

- updates,
- download legal forms,
- watch legal videos with a comic cast,
- learn from our free legal encyclopedia,
- connect with us on social media,
- and much more.